CLASSROOM
ENGAGEMENT

CLASSROOM ENGAGEMENT

The Unwritten Code

Jen Foster

1 Oliver's Yard
55 City Road
London EC1Y 1SP

2455 Teller Road
Thousand Oaks
California 91320

Unit No 323-333, Third Floor, F-Block
International Trade Tower
Nehru Place, New Delhi – 110 019

8 Marina View Suite 43-053
Asia Square Tower 1
Singapore 018960

Editor: Amy Thornton
Senior project editor: Chris Marke
Cover design: Wendy Scott
Typeset by: C&M Digitals (P) Ltd, Chennai, India

Library of Congress Control Number: 2025932274

British Library Cataloguing in Publication data

A catalogue record for this book is available from the British Library

ISBN 978-1-0362-0081-7
ISBN 978-1-0362-0080-0 (pbk)

Contents

About the author

Jen Foster is a fiercely passionate educator, trainer and consultant. Jen is the founder of The Good Morning Club which is the world's first online encylopedia for all things behaviour and beyond. Created by an educator for educators it includes bitesized training videos, bespoke resources and programmes as well as digital regulation tools. This research-backed, practical approach is now used in over 84 countries around the world. Jen is also the host of @goodmorningmsfosterltd where she supports over 150,000 educators with daily behaviour insights.

Kids do better when they are excited to come to class.

Bobbie French (2023)

Why this book and how to use it

WHY ENGAGEMENT?

For me, I am most engaged and in the moment when I am actually teaching. I am most unsettled inputting data *eye roll*. It will take me forever to do this task and I will find MANY ways to procrastinate (coffee anyone?).

In the most recent Department for Education (DfE) behaviour survey (May 2023), 25 per cent of teachers said pupil misbehaviour had led to ten minutes of time lost for every 30 minutes of lesson time (TES, 2024). A Teacher Tapp report shared that 62 per cent of primary school teachers in the most disadvantaged schools entirely stopped learning at least once in every lesson (Allen et al., 2024). With many of the schools I work with, we are seeing unsettled behaviour in lessons. Many articles and recommendations focus on cracking down on behaviour. But we are missing an undeniable variable: the learning. Think about the tasks you do at work and your behaviour associated with them. It is likely that your behaviour becomes more unsettled (notice I didn't say low-level behaviour!) the less interested you are in the content.

TAKE A MOMENT TO THINK ABOUT YOUR OWN ENGAGEMENT

- When are you most engaged at work?
- How does it then impact how you behave?

Think about your own:

- unsettled behaviour
- peak engagement.

Now, of course, there are going to be things that our children like more than others. However, I think we take for granted how much control we have over how we teach. The way we teach and the opportunities we provide have an enormous impact on how children engage with the learning. What if it wasn't just about the behaviour, but the variables that impact it? One of my favourite mantras is *control the controllables*.

But it's not just behaviour. In recent years, there has been a huge focus on attendance. Attendance rewards, parent fines and a continual narrative that attendance equals better results (Mediaofficer, 2023). But again, if we want our children to **want** to go to school, shouldn't we look a little deeper at the experience we are providing them? I mean, we know if there is a school trip our children are skipping in to start the day on time. How enriching is our daily offer?

We are also having a societal shift. As many as one in five children in the UK are neurodivergent, with the majority attending mainstream education (Conway, 2024). The core problem schools are facing is we have historically taught in a neurotypical way, expecting all children to sit, process and approach the task in the same way. This doesn't work for our classrooms which means lessons aren't flowing from A to B. More often than not children are not completing the work, disruptions are increasing and educators are left exhausted, repeating the same tired systems. Children are being labelled as 'disruptive', 'naughty' or having 'bad behaviour' when really it is more about them being unable to successfully access the work. Educators need to be given the practical tools to create neuroaffirming classrooms where all children can thrive, and YOU can enjoy the lesson too!

We have to talk about Covid. Covid-19 happened. There was a significant fracture to pupil learning and personal development. Once returning to school, educators felt a huge pressure to 'catch up' and close gaps, with big recommendations on tutoring and, again, attendance (Committee of Public Accounts, 2023). That was never going to be an easy time to navigate. But let's take a moment to touch down in **common sense town**. If we want children to do better, they need to enjoy what they are doing. Right?

If we want children to feel happier, to achieve more and to behave better, it seems to me that we need an engagement glow-up.

THE PURPOSE OF THIS BOOK

This book is about tackling the unwritten code of engagement. The missing part of the framework that undoubtedly influences how we feel, act and what we do.

WHAT TO EXPECT

Since this book is all about engagement, I have created it in a way that I hope is engaging to read! I mean, I can't stand it when you have school training about something and it is delivered in the opposite way. 'Let's talk about outdoor learning by watching three-hour videos online.'

This book is divided into Part 1 and Part 2. In Part 1, I have created each chapter to succinctly unpick the unwritten code of engagement. Most chapters follow the same structure.

You will see similar visuals; let me break it down:

Shift: An invitation to shift your mindset on engagement

Backspace: An opportunity to think about the historical change in narrative

Enter: The research you need to know

Loading: Still buffering? This section will answer those burning questions!

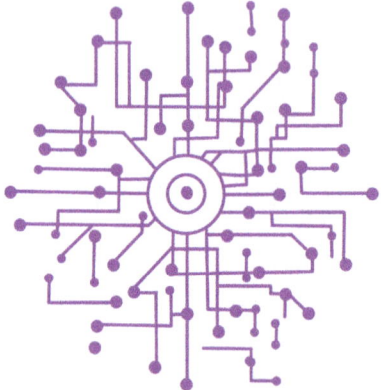

Links: Summarising how the chapter links to engagement

Floppy disc: The headlines to remember

Sim: Your notes area

There will also be regular opportunities for you to reflect and think about your experiences, so make sure you have a pen or pencil to hand! I actually love scribbling my thoughts on books, but I know some people find they have to keep them pristine! Please take this as your formal invitation to journal as you read! There is also a MAGICAL notes page at the back if you'd like to keep it contained!

Part 2 is all about the **how**. Again, HOW annoying is it when you're given the concepts but not the execution? I wanted this book to really and truly be your planning bestie. So, make sure you choose your school bag wisely with a clear compartment! Every idea is broken down in your magical manual so you have practical solutions, strategies and tasks at the ready. No gatekeeping. No blurred lines. Just you, me and engagement!

What is key is that nothing is a stand-alone strategy or concept. You will see central themes revisited and this is a good thing! Many of the strategies I share combine multiple areas of engagement. They might get children moving, but also get children collaborating and provide an alternative to no hands up all at the same time. I wanted to share the different layers of these activities to build your perspective throughout the book. As you work through it, you will be connecting the dots of how different threads of engagement build or complement others. It should be a holistic approach to engagement and you will experience that through each chapter.

In this book, you will be introduced to our MAGICAL framework for engagement. This is not a lesson plan or a tick box. Each element of the framework shares a different area of engagement to consider and reflect on with your classroom. This isn't about overwhelming you and creating a new to-do list. It is about providing a bank of ideas at your fingertips to adapt, tweak and inject that magic back into your lesson!

Finally, this book is yours for life. Yay! I have curated it to be returned to over and over again for inspiration and spark. Don't feel like you have to read it in one go. But I promise, each time you open it up you will have an idea at the ready.

Let's demystify engagement together for you and your kids!

Part

1

If a child can't learn the way we teach, maybe we should teach the way they learn.

Ignacio Estrada

CHAPTER 1

The engagement question: What is engagement? Why does it matter?

THEY TOLD ME THEY WERE OFF TASK. I ASKED THEM, 'WHAT WAS THE TASK?'

As a behaviour consultant and trainer, I am often asked about children struggling to stay focused on tasks. How can we incentivise them to focus? How can we teach focus or create routines to get children to focus? While these questions are instinctive – and are absolutely valid in the classroom – we also need to step back and ask: What are we actually asking them to focus on? Is the actual content 'focus worthy'? How often do we dwell on that question? I actually think one of the best indicators is how we feel when we are planning. We have all had that experience when we are planning a lesson and just think 'Oh my gosh, they are absolutely going to love this.' Equally, we have all trudged through a set of slides just to tick it off the list. Does it inspire us? Nope. Are we excited to teach it? Not really. A big misconception about engagement is that it takes more time, resourcing and energy. Hopefully, this book will debunk that myth for you and you will be skipping out of school earlier and enjoying teaching more!

Shift

THE ELEPHANT IN THE ROOM

'Engagement' is a term you have most likely heard many times; however, it is not one that gets a lot of air time. We rarely have staff meetings on engagement and I would be surprised if you've actually ever been given a definition or a shared vision for engagement. So, it would be a bit weird if we didn't address the elephant in the room, wouldn't it? Before we move on, let's tackle this beast. How would you describe engagement? What words come to mind? What pictures come to mind? Take a few minutes to just process what engagement means to you. Write in and around our elephant!

LET'S ADDRESS THE ELEPHANT IN THE ROOM

Figure 1.1   The elephant in the room

I asked some of my community and these are some of their ideas. Tick the ones that resonate with you!

- Children ask questions
- Children feel creative
- Children love learning
- Educators love teaching
- Children are full participants in their learning
- Play is involved!
- Curiosity is tapped into

- Children drive their learning
- Opportunities to approach learning in their own way
- When all voices are heard
- There is an excitement about learning
- Learning is accessible
- Children feel inspired
- There is a sense of involvement
- The learning ignites joy
- Children give their attention to the learning
- Children can participate in inclusive ways

YES to all of these! When we talk about engagement in this book we are referring to all of these wonderful ideas and aspirations. In order for children to be engaged, the content has to be something they can access and approach. Engagement conjures up those images of children with their tongue out super-focused and 'in the zone'. It is more than the initial spark, it is what keeps them engrossed. It isn't for a reward, it is for the process. Engaging lessons just feel joyful. We can guide our strategies for engagement with this definition:

Children are engaged when they feel <u>invited</u> into the learning and are <u>intrinsically inter-</u><u>ested</u> in exploring <u>further</u> and <u>remaining</u> on the learning task. Genuine engagement sparks genuine <u>joy</u>.

ENGAGEMENT IS A PSYCHOLOGICAL CONCEPT

Amy Berry (2022) shares that one of the most common ways of describing engagement comes from the field of educational psychology and research into human motivation. This looks at a positive connection and involvement with the task and categorises engagement as having three domains:

- *emotional engagement*: feeling enthusiastic, passionate and invested in the activity;
- *cognitive engagement*: paying close attention, actively thinking and problem-solving;
- *behavioural engagement*: putting in effort, persisting through challenges and going the extra mile.

However, as with all theories, it is always tricky to agree! There are other domains that have been proposed such as academic, social, collaborative and agentic (having some sort of agency in the task).

It is quite wordy, isn't it? The good news is, we cover all of these domains throughout your magical manual, so YAY!

THE ENGAGEMENT GAP

In the book *Engagement by Design* (Fisher et al., 2018), the authors emphasise that we must first tackle the engagement gap before anything else. Student engagement has been found to be a predictor of academic achievement, overall life satisfaction, decrease in unsafe behaviours and dropout rates.

I think we can safely say engagement is intrinsically linked to wellbeing, behaviour and academic outcomes. It can be helpful to think of it as the gravitational anchor in the school solar system!

REWARDS FRACTURE ENGAGEMENT

Eeek. I always hate to be the messenger here, but you won't find a chapter on extrinsic rewards in this book. Research from Dr Daniel Pink (2011) and Alfie Kohn (2018) highlights how when we use rewards for anything more than algorithmic tasks (i.e. line up or tuck your chair in), they reduce motivation within the task. This is a concept I often teach when training schools. I share that information and then I bring out some chocolates. Everyone straightens up. I tell educators that I will give them a series of tasks to get a chocolate bar. I start with simple, algorithmic tasks, such as stand up or put your hand on your head. I then increase the complexity and need for problem-solving – for example, can you tell me the two authors I referenced for motivation and write their full name on a whiteboard in cursive writing and in alphabetical order and hold it above your head?

As we 'play' this game lots of really interesting things happen:

- those who feel they can't, don't
- many get annoyed about not being seen
- it increases the noise level
- it reduces collaboration
- those who already have a chocolate or two don't care any more
- some educators do something different like their to-do list
- as chocolates begin to run out it becomes more frantic
- arguments happen
- some feel like they can't access if they are at the back/don't have a whiteboard etc.

Let's go back to our definition and switch it to adults:

> Adults are engaged when they feel _invited_ into the learning and are _intrinsically interested_ in exploring _further_ and _remaining_ on task. Genuine engagement sparks genuine _joy_.

Not everyone feels invited, it is purely for the chocolate, not anything else! It sparks more frenzy than joy! This is similar to what happens in classrooms across the world. We were sold a story of extrinsic motivators, but they are not the key to engagement.

ENGAGEMENT DOESN'T HAPPEN THROUGH STILLNESS

We will explore this more in Chapter 8 on movement, but let's agree to stop wasting time trying to get children to be statues. Stillness is not the marker for optimum engagement (NITB, 2023). When we do that, children are purely focusing on trying to be still rather than anything else. This isn't to say stillness is bad. Some children will revel with a bit of 'head on the desk time' or a lay down in the book corner. Some children may love to sit still to process. I know when I am reading something that I am super-engaged in I tend to 'croc out' and not move for hours! But let's emphasise 'some'. What we want to move away from is cookie-cutter systems for engagement. If you are spending your time waiting for everyone to sit a certain way in order to deem them 'engaged' then your focus has been misplaced.

ENGAGEMENT DOESN'T REQUIRE SILENCE

'Wow, what a lovely silent room, seems like everyone is super-focused.' Ever been praised for a silent room? Me too. And once again, there is NOTHING wrong with silent working. I love a bit of silence peppered throughout the day so I can hear my thoughts! But silence isn't the sole indicator for engagement. We will look more into this when we explore connection in Chapter 12, but, ultimately, if you've ever worked from home more than one day in a row you will know silence can feel deafening after a while! As humans we crave connection and conversation too (Barrett, 2021). We also need to remember some of our children might stim (such as humming or slightly tapping) in order to support regulation within the classroom environment (Rudy, 2024). For this reason, it is important that our classrooms take into account all learners' needs to shift the narrative of engagement.

Old truths		New truths
Children are static	→	Children engage through movement
Rewards motivate children to do the work	→	Deeper engagement requires more than surface-level rewards
Everyone doing the same things	→	Children are different and engagement looks different
The educator controls the tempo and the engagement	→	The children are equal partners in the lesson
Children are engaged when they are silent	→	Children engage in different ways

Old truths/new truths

HEADLINES TO REMEMBER ON ENGAGEMENT

- All children need to access in order to engage
- Children should feel intrinsically motivated when they are engaged
- Engagement feels joyful

YOUR NOTES ON ENGAGEMENT

Note down three things you want to remember from this chapter and take forward into your teaching and classroom.

When students are engaged and connect learning with their everyday lives, they are 14 times more likely to be academically motivated.

Fisher et al. (2018)

CHAPTER 2

Activate MAGICAL engagement

HOW ARE WE MEASURING ENGAGEMENT?

Eww. I don't mean making judgements, but we do need an engagement indicator. If not, how do we know if children are engaged? It is important to look at engagement as a whole-class concept as well as an individual one. This is worth our time because we often skip engagement, jump to behavioural difficulties or academic struggles and miss a fundamental variable. Are children engaged? Here's what engagement might look and feel like in a lesson:

- children are actively doing the task/learning
- children ask relevant questions
- children seek out challenges
- there is a fluidity in the task, children move through steps/stages enthusiastically
- children look and feel in control, changing their work position, getting equipment they need, discussing with their partner where needed
- classroom talk centres around the learning/task
- children share their own experiences/ideas linked to the learning/task
- children approach the task with flexibility, some children working quietly or independently while others naturally work collaboratively
- children seem 'in flow' and lost in the task
- children seem regulated; while they may be excited, the classroom seems calm rather than frantic
- children can access tools to support continued regulation, i.e. chair bands or fidgets
- children want to continue the learning and ask to do more/if they can have extra time
- children are focused on the learning and are not distracted.

This can be a great checklist to use to measure the engagement of your class or a specific child. I also think it is helpful to identify what disengagement looks like. Again, having this criteria can be helpful to build discussions around what behaviour is communicating, how to accelerate pupil progress and develop a positive culture in the classroom. If children (or a child) are disengaged you might see children:

- not starting the work
- not staying on task
- asking for help with minimal tasks, i.e. writing the date
- asking to leave the classroom or their seat, i.e. to sharpen a pencil, get some water, go to the toilet (repeatedly)
- talking, not about the learning or the task
- frequently distracted
- seemingly dysregulated; this might be a head on a desk, signs of frustration, shouting, snapping etc.
- glazed over
- unable to explain or discuss the learning/task
- looking and feeling trapped in their seat or with the task, maybe throwing or sliding things on the floor, rocking on their chair, banging etc.
- showing signs of a stress response like hiding under a desk, seemingly aggressive or leaving their seat
- stop and starting with the task
- asking when it is finished/when lunch is.

TAKE A MOMENT TO THINK ABOUT ENGAGEMENT INDICATORS

Take a moment to think about the engagement of your class. How would you measure it? Consider these three types of indicators:

- Behavioural indicators
- Cognitive indicators
- Emotional indicators

These can be helpful reflective activities when you've had 'one of those days'. There is something I always talk about when it comes to education and that is 'audience narrative'. It basically means that it is easier to understand something when you are looking at it from the outside perspective. It is super-hard to problem-solve when you're in the thick of it. That is why we always give the best advice to our friends and family, but find it impossible to see a solution when it concerns us! This is where checklists can come in handy, so fold this page and come back to it when you need to gain a bit of audience narrative on what is happening with your class.

INTRODUCING THE MAGICAL FRAMEWORK

This book is not about giving you a slice. It is the whole damn pie. So, we know engagement levels have dipped, and we want to do something about it. Say BONJOUR to the MAGICAL framework. This is the breakdown of research-backed concepts for engagement. This is not a tick list. I repeat, this is <u>not</u> a tick list. We don't want to see a new wave of lesson plans with a box for each area for magical engagement. That would be a Greek tragedy. This is about delivering a holistic understanding of engagement as well as practical activities at your fingertips. Unlike traditional books, this book comes with your very own MAGICAL manual. So, you can read about the concept and then hand-pick what activities you'd like to include in your lesson. Can I get a *woop woop*?

MAGICAL ENGAGEMENT BREAKDOWN

Think of magical engagement as a wheel of possibilities and inspiration. Spin and add some sparkle to your lesson. There isn't an order you need to work through; in fact, it is personal to you. You might read the framework and build an order you like to work through in your MAGICAL notes section. But what do they all mean?

Element of magical engagement	In a nutshell
Movement	Moving is essential!
A task not an ask	Increase participation by removing hands up
Game time	Play is children's universal love language
Intrinsic motivation	Keep children motivated
Connection	We crave social connections
Attune	We need to be regulated to learn
Ladder	How to remain engaged and on task when things feel challenging

Element of magical engagement

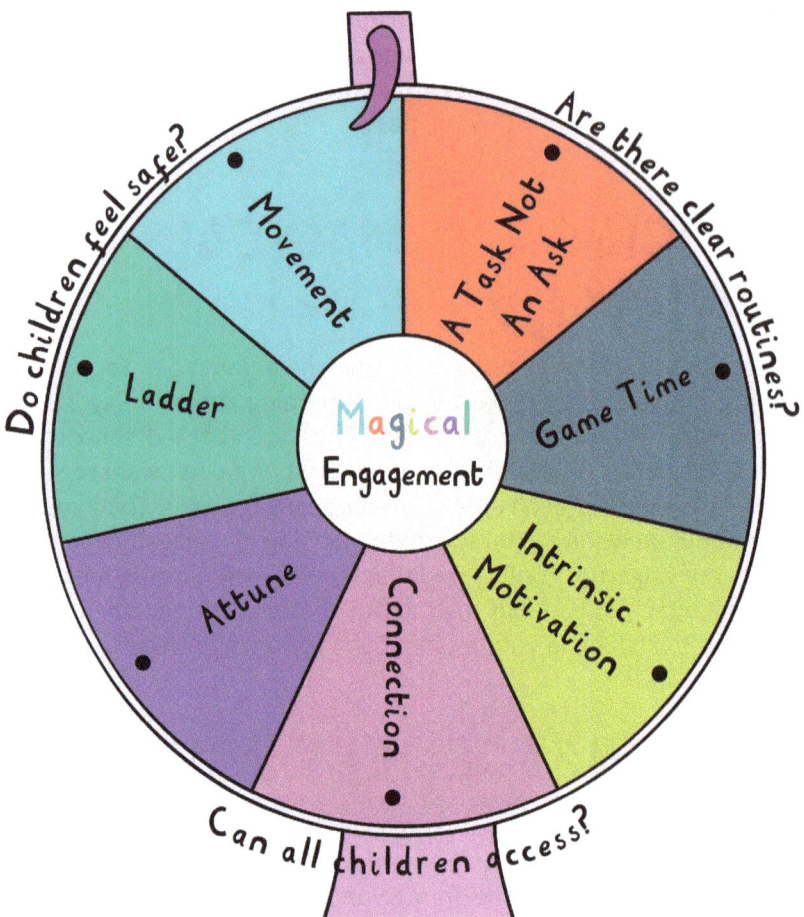

Figure 2.1   Wheel of engagement

There are many systems in schools, but, arguably, some of the most fundamental influences on learning, behaviour and wellbeing lack systems. They are left in a grey area. If we want to see a shift in the 'engagement gap' we need to shift our dialogue around it. This flowchart is not perfect and far from exhaustive, but it is a starting point to analysing what is happening in your classroom and what might help! I don't know about you, but on the days, I need it most I am looking for fast-track navigation, not profound problem-solving!

Magical Engagement Navigation

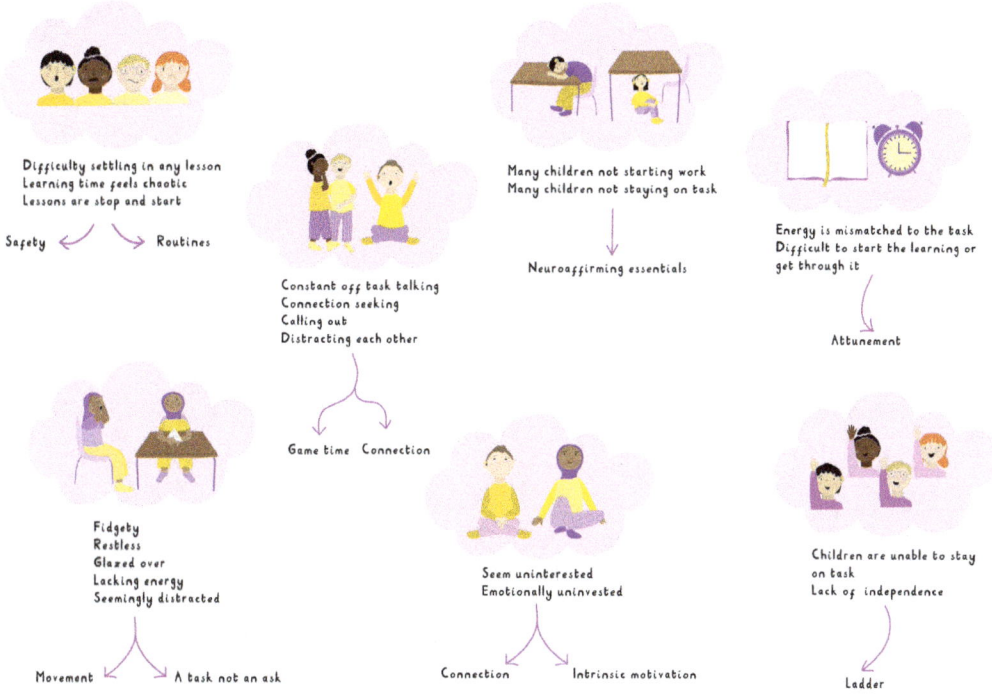

Figure 2.2   Magical engagement navigation

YOUR NOTES ON MAGICAL ENGAGEMENT

An unmet need remains unmet until it's met.

Naish and Dillon (2020)

CHAPTER 3

Safety before magic

SAFETY BEFORE MAGICAL ENGAGEMENT

'But Jen, how did you manage to sit through that staff meeting?'

That was the response from my deputy head as I burst into tears. I had just informed her that during dismissal another adult was aggressive towards me. I was 21 at the time and absolutely terrified. I was shaking and couldn't stop thinking about it. But I had to go straight into a staff meeting. I can't tell you what that staff meeting was about. But I can tell you I spent the entire time trying not to cry. Here's the thing: you cannot begin to engage with something if you don't feel safe.

This might seem like an extreme example, but for our children unsafety wears many hats. Think of our experiences as a library. We have a negative bias towards unsafe or unknown experiences as our evolutionary mindset is driven to keep us safe. Our brain needed to remember if berries were poisonous and needed to be vigilant of paths unknown – strictly survival purposes. For our children's developing brains, so much of their library is in the unknown shelves. Which means, they step into our classrooms *needing* to feel safe. This is their primary and most important need.

Why am I talking about this? Because we simply cannot begin to talk about engagement until children feel safe. We cannot delve into the realms of magical engagement until we have laid the foundations of security.

TIPPING CHAIRS

Victor used to enter my classroom by tipping chairs. The first 'lesson' (air quotes intended) he engaged in was such a surprise to me. It was a maths addition booklet. Barely a lesson really! I turned it into one because he seemed so calm. He sat and completed the whole booklet. He was far more engaged than any of my *all singing, all dancing* lessons. Why? Because Victor was experiencing a stress response. He was in a state of hypervigilance and adding unknown bells and whistles to that only escalated him further. Creating a sense of repetition, predictability and calm felt safe.

When I was a senior leader and class teacher, I was out of class more than I'd like to be. When I returned, I felt like I could barely get through a lesson. I finally realised this was because my class felt so anxious not knowing when I was coming or going and who would be teaching them. I was able to support them to feel safe by sharing really clear, visual information and removing the unknown! Maybe there is a time your lesson wasn't quite getting to the lesson part? Perhaps it was during transition time or before the holidays.

TAKE A MOMENT TO CONSIDER SAFETY

- Have you ever had a child who was trickier to engage with than others?

  - Was there a background of trauma?
  - Which lessons did they engage with most?

- What about your whole class? Think about times that have felt turbulent.

  - Can you trace a link back to safety and security?
  - Can you think of a time when your class were collectively unsettled?
  - How do you think it might have been linked to their sense of safety?

WAIT, BACK UP A SECOND. THERE'S AN ELEPHANT IN THE ROOM

You see, when I asked thousands of teachers if safety was important in their school there was an overwhelming and resounding yes. But here's the elephant. When we talk about safety in school, we often refer to safeguarding. Something we have regular training on, something that underlies every policy and is categorically the most important thing we do. So what's the problem?

Safety is our top priority. But what about security? Read that again.

A child's safety and *sense* of safety are different things. Safety is (rightly so) paramount to everything we do. But a child's sense of safety is not always central to discussions. A child's sense of safety is the first stepping stone to learning. We might call this their sense of security, to differentiate. This refers to their psychological feeling of safety which, of course, in turn, impacts them physically (DOAC, 2024).

Why do we need to prioritise a child's sense of security?

COGNITIVE LOAD THEORY

Imagine your brain as a computer. It's got a limited amount of RAM, right? Are we loving all of these technology analogies gang? Well, that's kind of like our working memory. When we're trying to learn something new, our brain uses up a lot of that RAM.

Now, imagine your classroom as a computer program. If that program is always crashing or running slowly, it's not going to work very well. Similarly, if a classroom is chaotic and unpredictable, our children's brains are constantly working overtime to figure out what's going on.

Cognitive load theory highlights the importance of predictable routines to support children to feel safe, allowing children to focus on learning new concepts and skills (Reese et al., 2016).

WE CAN'T LEARN IF OUR NEEDS AREN'T MET

Most of us are pretty familiar with Maslow's 'hierarchy of needs' influenced by the Blackfoot nation. This image shows a slightly adapted version that makes direct parallels to education. This theory illustrates how, as humans, we are motivated to fulfil our needs. Ultimately, needs lower down in the hierarchy must be satisfied before individuals can attend to needs higher up. As I dropped my son off at school this morning, I overheard a child say to their parent: 'Are you sure I will be able to go for a poo before carpet time?' If a child's basic safety or belonging needs are not met, we cannot expect optimum engagement within the lesson. You might have hit the rest of the magical framework, but if a child needs the toilet, that is going to be the only thing they are thinking about. Similarly to Chapter 13 on attunement, this doesn't mean we have to be a mind reader! In our magical manual we will outline practical classroom resources to support children to communicate their needs to you.

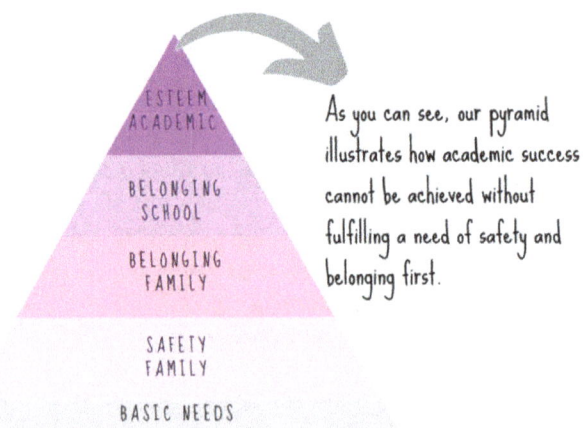

As you can see, our pyramid illustrates how academic success cannot be achieved without fulfilling a need of safety and belonging first.

Figure 3.1   Pyramid of needs

BODY BUDGET

Dr Emma Hepburn (2023) visualises neuroscience and highlights how our brains are constantly predicting based on our sensations, our environment, other people, emotions, experiences and well ... everything. Why does this matter and have anything to do with engagement? Well, our brain is constantly predicting, making judgements and organising resources on what our body needs. It is CONSTANTLY surveying for possible threats. So, if our children detect a whiff of danger all of the body's resources get redirected to dealing with that. Regardless of there being a real-life danger or not. Our body doesn't differentiate. This puts engaging with the task on the back burner and safety at the top of the to-do list. This marries perfectly with our understanding of the stress response.

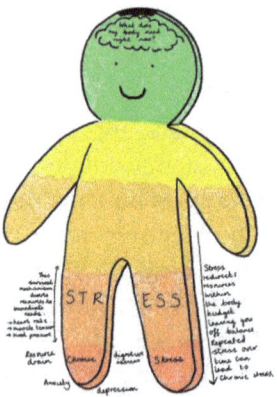

Figure 3.2   What does my body need right now?

(adapted from Hepburn, 2023)

UNDERSTANDING THE STRESS RESPONSE

When feelings become overwhelming, and we get dysregulated, this can trigger a stress response in the body.

Figure 3.3   Dysregulation refers to being in a state of emotional, mental and physical imbalance

Children feel these more deeply. Why? Their prefrontal cortex isn't fully formed yet. So that rational thought is still developing. Children have fewer experiences to fall back on and therefore don't actually know if it is going to be 'okay'. Our experiences help to wire our responses. The more unknown, the more triggers. It is so important to note that a stress response is an involuntary physiological reaction. Words, threats or bribes won't bring children out of it. Treating it like 'misbehaviour' will only accelerate the stress. **The bottom line is: if a child is experiencing a stress response they will not be engaged in the task.** And actually, these are much more common than you think in your classroom.

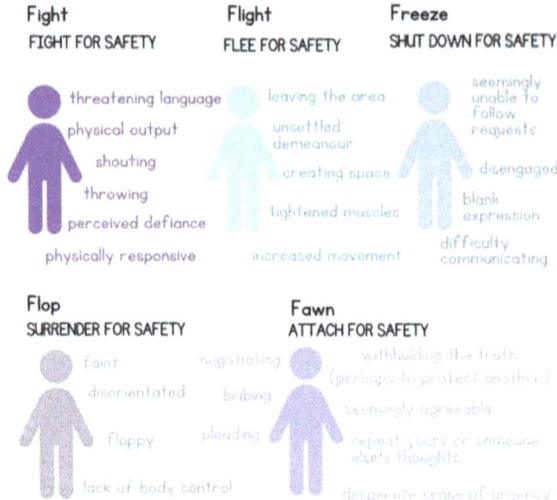

Figure 3.4   Fight, flight, freeze

Stress responses may be triggered by a child not being able to tie their laces and they have just become undone on the carpet. A child worried about taking their jumper off and their top coming off too. A child worrying about whether they are going to be asked a question on the spot. If they don't know who they are working with, if they have their lunchbox, what their lunch is, where they are sitting, who the adult is, if they have to perform, feedback, complete a task they find tricky like writing, be asked to read out loud in front of the class. That is why stress responses must be part of the conversation when we are talking about engagement in the classroom.

STRESS AND THE BRAIN

There are different levels of impact when it comes to emotions, regulation and engagement. We've looked at needs and stress, and it makes sense to finish on chronic stress. Chronic stress happens when we experience a stress response for a prolonged time. This was what Victor was experiencing. As Dr Wendy Suzuki states:

> *Stress releases stress hormones that go into the brain, at too high a level or too constant; it damages neural connections and then kills cells so it is intertwined.*

> The Diary of A CEO (2024)

If we want children to truly engage with a task, we need to cultivate environments where children feel safe and their needs are met.

THE ESCALATION CYCLE

The escalation cycle is an important reference because here we can understand how a child's regulation correlates with their possible engagement. We can all understand that a child isn't going to engage with the lesson if they are at peak dysregulation (Place2Be, 2024). But, looking at the image below, we also need to consider the build-up and the aftermath of peak dysregulation. We need to think about engagement from a regulation perspective. Remember that staff meeting I had to sit through? Investing in regulation **is** investing in engagement.

The Escalation Cyle
pattern occuring before, during and after a meltdown

- peak
- acceleration
- de-escalation
- agitation
- trigger
- calm
- recovery

Figure 3.5   Pattern of the escalation cycle

THINKING THROUGH QUESTIONS ON SAFETY IN THE CLASSROOM

HOW DO I MANAGE A BIG STRESS RESPONSE AS WELL AS TEACH?

Yes, I personally found this incredibly problematic as a class teacher. Which is why I developed resources and strategies to make this possible even without a teaching assistant. We will unpick these in the magical manual!

(Continued)

WHAT CAN I DO TO MAKE A CHILD FEEL SAFE AND SECURE SO THAT THEY CAN LEARN?

Safety is established through consistency, predictability and connection. We will unpick some everyday routines in the magical manual! These are particularly important in the first six weeks of school. This is a critical time when there are many unknown elements. This part of the manual is essential to securing that safe foundation.

HOW DO I KNOW IF A CHILD ISN'T REGULATED?

In our magical manual we share check-ins you can use with your class. This is a systematic way to quite literally 'check-in' with how pupils are feeling.

WHAT IF ONE OR TWO CHILDREN AREN'T REGULATED, WHAT SHOULD I DO?

Teaching is fricking hard enough, isn't it? This isn't about teaching 12 lessons at a time or running a boutique hotel with a menu of different activities. No. This is not about making your job any harder. This is about understanding that if children aren't regulated, they won't engage. So, if we strip this back, the question is, how do we get that (or those) children regulated? It's not by expecting them to just **do** the lesson. It's by giving them an opportunity to rest and reset within the classroom. This might be utilising a calm space, giving them a fidget, a few minutes' quiet in the reading corner or some free doodling on a whiteboard. There are many things we can do to support regulation. This isn't about putting a plaster on it; it's about utilising your toolbox. Or, in our case, your manual! I will share some 'on the spot' regulation strategies you can use with your children in your magical manual.

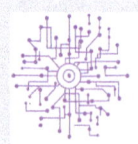

SAFETY ‣ ENGAGEMENT

Children will not engage if they don't feel safe.

HEADLINES TO REMEMBER FOR SAFETY IN THE CLASSROOM

- How often are we talking about a child's sense of security?
- If a child doesn't feel safe and secure, they cannot engage
- Regulation comes first

YOUR NOTES ON SAFETY

Note down three things you want to remember from this chapter and take forward into your teaching and classroom.

You do not rise to the level of your goals, you fall to the level of your systems.

James Clear (2018)

The path to magical engagement is routines!

CHAPTER 4

'I just don't see how it's going to work ...'

A conversation I had with my partner teacher in my first term of teaching. Believe it or not, I didn't want to turn the class into a courtroom. I didn't want to do a big drama activity. I didn't even want to have them out of their seats. Why? Because I was freaking out about classroom management! I didn't know how to manage everyone out of their seats, and if I didn't know, I wasn't up for it. Much like our kids to be honest! It is pretty embarrassing to admit and have it down on paper. But I was more comfortable when I felt I had control of the classroom. There, I said it. It took a while for me to branch out into engaging strategies and there was one thing I needed to master first. Routines.

Last chapter we looked at safety and the importance of having a foundational sense of security in the classroom. Routines are like the paving to that foundation, leading to magical engagement! Routines create a sense of security while establishing efficient classroom management. This is needed when we are using engaging activities where we are loosening the reins of control!

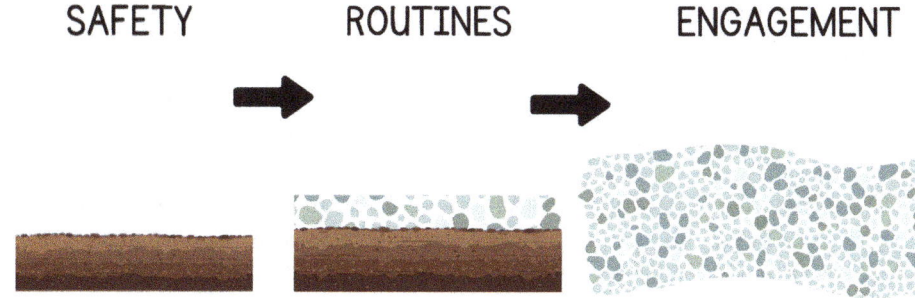

SAFETY **ROUTINES** **ENGAGEMENT**

Figure 4.1   Safety, routines, engagement

TWO FOR ONE

Whenever I lead a training day, I try to do a **two for one**. I have the content that I am using for training, but I **try** to deliver it with magical engagement. This always provides a perfect LIVE demonstration of the need for routines. Let me explain: something as (seemingly) simple as 'choose someone to write' sets off a hustle and bustle that can rival Oxford Circus.

You have the best handwriting … No, the pen was near you … I am really slow at writing … Anyone but me! … You know you want to do it …

Which delightfully derails my activity and allows me to share the importance of routines. The activity can't start if the routines are rusty. Simple as that. And the activity can't play out if the routines slow it down. Check out this difference …

Later in the day, I put a pen directly in front of someone on each table. I say, if you have a pen in front of you, hold it up in the air. Great, you are writing for this activity. And the activity begins.

TAKE A MOMENT TO THINK ABOUT A TIME WHEN A ROUTINE TOOK WAY TOO LONG

- What was the routine?
- What activity were you trying to do?
- How did it derail the activity?

WAIT, BACK UP A SECOND. ROUTINES AREN'T NEW

You can find routines in the *Teachers' Standards* in Teacher Standard 7 (DfE, 2021, p. 12). Quick refresh because obviously we don't know it off by heart now, do we?

… have clear rules and routines for behaviour in classrooms, and take responsibility for promoting good and courteous behaviour both in classrooms and around the school, in accordance with the school's behaviour policy

As well as the *Early Career Framework* (DfE, 2019, p. 22):

> **Establish effective routines and expectations, by:**
> - **Creating and explicitly teaching routines in line with the school ethos that maximise time for learning (e.g. setting and reinforcing expectations about key transition points).**
> - **Practising routines at the beginning of the school year.**
> - **Reinforcing routines (e.g. by articulating the link between time on task and success).**

I LOVE that we have got a mention of maximising that learning. YES. Now here's where we sometimes go wrong. Sometimes the routines become more about control rather than engagement. Paul Dix (2017) says that habits shouldn't restrict freedom, they should create it. And THAT is what we want to focus on. How can we utilise robust routines to make a gateway for engaging strategies? When it comes to routines, it is not about bringing something new to the table. It is about rethinking how they can enhance engagement.

SOCIAL CONTAGION

The idea that if everyone else is doing it, I'll do it as well. Ever gone into a quiet place like a library or study room and immediately lowered your voice? Ever entered a dance floor and started nodding your head? We are influenced by the people around us (Christakis and Fowler, 2011). Robust routines support that classroom management with the natural pied piper effect. Meaning, we can focus more on engagement and less on firefighting.

COGNITIVE LOAD

If we want to support our children to focus and engage, we need to lighten the load. As we learnt from our chapter on safety, our brain is constantly predicting. Predictable routines support our brain to hop on to autopilot. This means our precious cognitive resources can be redirected to learning. This closely links with anxiety.

REDUCE ANXIETY

Without the Ts crossed and the Is dotted, it doesn't really make sense, does it? If we don't know the ins and outs of something it can cause anxiety. Anxiety is when we are consumed by the thought of the unknown. As beautifully stated in *The Inclusive Classroom*:

For many children, just entering the classroom with its wide range of unpredictable events, interactions and expectations is a huge source of anxiety, which impacts their learning, behaviour and wellbeing.

Sobel and Alston (2021)

When children know the systems, they aren't walking into the room or the lesson blindfolded. They have regular cues of safety and consistency. James Clear said it brilliantly:

Goals are about the results you want to achieve. Systems are about the processes that lead to those results.

(2018)

Our routines pave the way for engagement!

THE PATHWAY TO FLOW

Flow (which comes up a few times in this book) is essentially what happens when we become so completely engaged with what we're doing, all ideas or worries dissolve and we're just completely present in the task. When we have robust systems in our classroom our mind and body naturally fall into flow with a lot more ease. Routines support your class to understand different prompts which take the *thinking* element out where it's not needed! When we don't stop and start, we can engage easier.

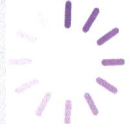 **HOW LONG DOES IT TAKE TO TEACH A ROUTINE?**

It takes 21 days to form a habit they said. It (unfortunately) isn't true (Selk, 2021). I know, I loved the idea of one month to the finish line. But it was a myth that gained A LOT of traction. Anyone else buy a 21-day journal? Just me? Okay.

So, you're probably waiting for the answer. Well, James Clear (2020) shares that it takes 66 days on average. But we also have to take into account the type of routine, how often they are likely to do it each day, how it is framed, the clarity of the routine ... I mean. I could go on. There are so many variables. I don't want you to get disheartened though. Let's reframe. Instead of racing to a goal of finishing teaching routines, let's focus on how we *continually* teach routines for daily success. This isn't as hellish as it sounds. In the magical manual I will share six easy, low-resource games you can play to ensure routines are always tip top!

HOW MANY ROUTINES DO I NEED TO TEACH?

I think of routines as reading between the lines of the school day. Everything children need to do automatically that isn't necessarily on your lesson plan. In terms of engagement there are a few routine 'pain points'. Think MAAT.

- *Movement between tasks*: how will children get equipment, walk around the room etc.
- *Assignment*: who is doing what? Let's not forget the pen!
- *Attention getters*: how will you stop children effectively?
- *Transition instructions*: if they are already in the depth of a task, how can we share instructions effectively?

We will share practical ideas for MAAT routines in your magical manual!

WHAT IF MY ROUTINE IS STILL TAKING AGES?

It might not be the right routine. I used to have a song for children to hand out whiteboards. It was in the tune of London Bridge is Falling Down and they would pass the whiteboards down and sing the tune. The class I created it with NAILED IT every time. They loved it and it brought some energy into the class as well as everyone having their equipment.

The next class I tried it with just didn't love it. There would be a handful of children singing. Some would scream, whiteboards would be everywhere, sometimes it was just children chatting. It didn't matter how many times I positively practised it. The routine wasn't routineing.

If it's not working, it isn't your fault or their fault. You'll know it's not working if you haven't really had a successful run at it. Just switch it up. In my case, I set the whiteboards at the back of the room and asked children row by row to collect in a clockwise route around the classroom. I know it sounds pedantic. But honestly, it worked!

HOW CAN I RETEACH ROUTINES IN A CROWDED CURRICULUM?

RIGHT? Luckily our games are five minutes or less that I will share in the magical manual. Remember, if routines are rusty, the efficiency of the lesson suffers too. So, investing in routines definitely pays off!

WHAT IF ONLY A FEW CHILDREN AREN'T FOLLOWING THE ROUTINES?

I get this a lot. What we need to remember is robust routines will have a social contagion effect. If most children are doing it, they will generally tag along. If a few children aren't that is an anomaly and indicates that there is something more going on with the child rather than the routine. Work with your senior leaders to put a plan of support in place to identify the why.

SAFETY + ROUTINES = ENGAGEMENT

HEADLINES TO REMEMBER ON ROUTINES

- Routine removes the hassle of engagement
- Routines make children feel safe
- The road to engagement is paved with routines!

YOUR NOTES ON ROUTINES

Note down three things you want to remember from this chapter and take forward into your teaching and classroom.

_____

_____

_____

_____

You are contagious.

Vanessa Van Edwards (2017)

CHAPTER 5

Body check

In my second year of teaching I had a student teacher. Which was absolutely wild to me. I had no idea how to be a grown up. I was barely one myself at the time. I didn't think I would have anything to teach him, but just cracked on business as usual. As we sharpened pencils after school one day he turned to me with a look of disbelief. 'How the HELL did you do that without talking?' Obviously, I had no clue what he was talking about, I was far more invested in counting equipment and checking labels on pencil cases. He went on: 'After lunch, I don't think you said anything for like, 20 minutes?'

He was right. I had clocked on pretty early that lunch time was an extremely heightened experience for my nine-year-olds. Trying to teach a lesson straight away was like stepping into rough waves without waiting for the tide to settle – you'll struggle to find your footing and the lesson risks being swept away (along with your new sunglasses) before it begins.

But this isn't about attunement – more of that in our magical framework. This was about the power of body language.

I would line children up outside the class (as per policy). Walk up and down and give children a smile, I would act out a book sign (where is my charades gang at?) for children to collect from their bag. I would then use gestures to usher children into the room quietly and start reading. I would often touch children on the shoulder to just give that extra sense of safety and belonging. I had music on in the classroom and children would read for about 15 minutes.

If I can calm a class of 30 nine-year-olds after lunch without speaking, surely we can use our body language to engage too?

As educators there is generally a point in the day where we are talking and it would be absolutely fantastic if children could listen. Whether you are a nursery practitioner conducting a circle time, a classroom teacher sharing the activity or a lecturer at the front of an auditorium. At some point, you're talking and they are (fingers crossed) listening. What if we could harness our body language to rapidly increase engagement within our delivery?

WHAT KEEPS YOU HOOKED?

In our digital world of scrolling, what keeps you hooked? Can you maintain focus for a 90-second Instagram reel? Because there is a whole industry right now that focuses on how creators engage their audience and increase their watch time. The next time you open your phone to do some consuming (no judgement here, my friend), just notice, notice when you watch three seconds and swipe down. Notice when you lock in and stay locked in. Maybe even pause and pop on your phone now. Permission granted! If we struggle to stay engaged, it seems pretty worthwhile reflecting on how we deliver information in the classroom.

WAIT, BACK UP A SECOND

When I think back to life at primary school I remember many educators sitting at desks. I don't remember being captivated. It was giving Victorian England. But my son came home this week and said, 'Mummy! There is something very suspicious in our school woods! Mr May found a curious item. But don't worry, we have CLUES!' It was so obvious, the way he was telling me, was the way it was delivered. He was PUMPED. When I asked my community of thousands of teachers 100 per cent of them said they have never had a training on body language. Rather than leaving this level 10 engagement to a lottery, why don't we start actually spilling the tea on the impact of our body language and engagement?

WHAT DO I MEAN BY BODY LANGUAGE?

Before I share some of the research, let's unpick the elements of body language. Body language is:

- expressions, including micro-expressions
- eye contact
- posture
- gestures
- proximity

- touch
- body movements
- head movements
- tone and pace of voice.

Well, that is one busy body, am I right?

GESTURES

Vanessa Van Edwards (2017) studied thousands of Ted Talks. She looked at the viral Ted Talks vs the least views. One of her key findings from this research was that the most viral Ted Talks used more gestures. More specifically, they used 475 in comparison to 272 in 18 minutes. She shares that our brain gives 12.5 x MORE WEIGHT to gestures than words. When gestures are used effectively, they should **underline** your content (more of this in your magical manual).

PATTERN DIFFERENCE

Julian Treasure (n.d.) came on to the Ted Talk stage and played white noise. He said, if I kept that on for two minutes while I was speaking you would soon cease to hear it. Because it is the same, constant sound, we naturally tune it out. I noticed this all the time when I was teaching, as soon as I saw some glazed faces I would change my voice. Maybe I moved to a whisper, maybe I went a bit louder, maybe I changed the actual tone rather than the volume. This creates a sense of focus and engagement and breaks through (what could be) white noise!

BODY TALKS

We can also create pattern difference with our positioning and proximity. Albert Mehrabian shared the 7/38/55 model (experianta, n.d.):

- 7 per cent of our communication is words;
- 38 per cent is vocal;
- 55 per cent is non-verbal.

How are we using our body to engage children? Is it mirroring what we are delivering? Is it enhancing connection? (More in your magical framework!)

I'M EXCITED

Vanessa Van Edwards shared a brilliant case study in her Ted Talk (2017). They asked students to perform a singing accuracy test. They had three control groups. The first group came in and just sang. The second said 'I'm nervous' before they started. The third said 'I'm excited' before they started. Guess what? The group who said they were excited were 80 per cent accurate. More than 20 per cent more accurate than the 'nervous' group. Why am I sharing this? Because how you feel shows in your body language. And we are spreading it in our lessons. If you are not engaged about what you are teaching, it is highly likely they won't be.

 **BUFFERING THOUGHTS**

DO I HAVE TO BE CONSTANTLY PERFORMING?

Of course not! This isn't about preparing an accompanying dance routine to perfectly complement your lesson. It is just about 'underlining' your messaging through your gestures and body language

DO I ALWAYS HAVE TO STAND UP?

Not at all! Pattern difference is about changing it up to keep attention and engagement. Moving from a standing position to sitting on a chair is a version of that. What we don't want to do is too much of anything. If we are constantly walking around, that is distracting. If we are constantly sitting down, that begins to feel passive. If we are constantly standing in one place, it feels robotic.

WHAT IF IT DOESN'T COME NATURALLY TO ME?

I hear that! This chapter is about understanding the gravity of our body language when it comes to our communication. Our body is communicating to our children whether we like it or not. I personally feel more empowered when I am aware of the impact I can have in the classroom. If it feels like a personality shift, start with the 1 per cent. Maybe it is just showing the number whenever you say it. Maybe it is also linking that to **movement** and **a task not an ask**. Where children do it too! Small changes, big impact. That is the kind of energy I am here for.

CAN IT REALLY INCREASE MY PUPIL ENGAGEMENT?

If you went to a training session and the person sat in one position or stood in one position with their hands behind their back and in the same pace and tone of voice the whole time … how long would you listen for? It matters!

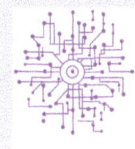

THE ENGAGEMENT ALGORITHM

Engaged body = Engaged learners

Your body is doing most of the teaching; is it engaging your learners?

HEADLINES TO REMEMBER ON BODY CHECK

- Your voice is just 7 per cent of what you are saying
- We read gestures 12.5 x faster than words

YOUR NOTES ON BODY CHECK

Note down three things you want to remember from this chapter and take forward into your teaching and classroom.

_____

_____

_____

_____

_____

_____

_____

_____

The real driver of attention and achievement in education is nourishing curiosity.

Sir Ken Robinson (2018)

The store cupboard

'Oh my gosh, we have a whole bunch of labels! They will love that. Storyboard with labels?'

Every time my partner teacher and I felt like the lesson was a bit dry we would take it to the store cupboard. We looked through what humble resources we had and how we could link them to the learning or make them part of the task. Because we all know, a touch of novelty and curiosity ignites a spark of excitement.

As Amy Berry (2022) says, 'At the risk of pointing out the obvious, it is hard to get motivated and excited about an inherently boring task.' There are so many times I have looked through my planning and thought, nah, this ain't it. If I am not excited about teaching it, I cannot begin to expect my class to be excited about learning it. This is around about the same time I would start rustling in the cupboard! As Martin Seligman says, 'The opposite end of the dimension of curiosity is being easily bored' (2011). Although we don't want to 'shield' children from this emotion, we certainly don't want it to be the theme tune for our curriculum.

Now, as a consultant, I discuss this with school leaders. If you do a learning walk, and you can't remember anything about the lesson or weren't invested to find out more, how can we expect our kids to be?

Curiosity is such a key ingredient to engagement and yet it seems to be left out of the 'non-negotiables' (pass the bucket) when it comes to lesson planning and expectations.

Curiosity will be woven throughout the MAGICAL framework and activities but let's get into some humble resources that are just on the other side of your cupboard doors. Have you ever bought a cooking book? They normally have a section like 'freezer stash' or 'equipment checklist'. This section is your visual store cupboard. A reminder of all of the ways you can add some PIZAZZ (LOVE this word) into your lessons.

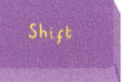

AN INTEGRAL ELEMENT OF ENGAGEMENT

Let me show you an integral element of engagement. You will need all your brain power, so if it's 9.30pm on a school night … maybe fold this page and come back to it tomorrow. But, if you think you are up for it, read on, my friend.

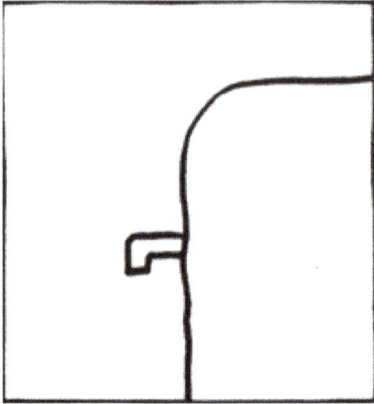

Figure 6.1   Mystery image

Look at this image. Really look at it. Maybe set your time for 60 seconds before you attempt to guess what it is.

What do you think this is?

Now, if you're still here, you're probably feeling pretty invested, right? WHAT IS IT? When is she going to tell us? What does it even mean?

Well, in all honesty, it was just an experiment. It was merely an example of how curiosity shifts our mindset and energy. But also, did you notice how I set it up? I told you it was important and that it would need a certain type of mindset to approach it. It's likely that made you want to read on and intrigued you. THIS is what curiosity does in the classroom and it is so ridiculously simple AND overlooked.

Oh, the picture? It is a submarine going over a waterfall. Obviously. Ha! (Barrett, 2021).

If anyone needs any convincing, here are five truths about curiosity.

1   If teachers can keep the flow of curiosity burning in children then pretty much everything else will follow from there (Robinson, 2018).
2   Curiosity is often described as the thirst for knowledge, a natural trait that propels children to explore and learn. Research has consistently shown that curious students perform better academically (Shah et al., 2018).
3   Dr Matthias Gruber (2015) explains that this is because curiosity puts the brain in a state that allows it to learn and retain any kind of information, like a vortex that sucks in what you are motivated to learn, and also everything around it.

4   Curious students not only ask questions but also actively seek out the answers (Stenger, 2014).
5   We can think about curiosity as the psychological equivalent of a healthy heartbeat (Gerlach, 2023).

Sparking curiosity is one of the easiest tweaks we can make to a lesson. A ripped piece of paper with a missing message, a mystery object, a mark on the floor to investigate, a sneak peek of a front cover … it isn't about creating elaborate classroom scenes (although obviously this is great too!) … it's about prompting questions, integrating elements of surprise or novelty and a desire to 'solve'.

THIS is what your **engagement store cupboard** is all about. Humble resources serving high impact! You will see items from the engagement store cupboard in every chapter and linked to different aspects of our framework. Think of this as your landing page. Go ahead and bookmark your visual cupboard. Is anyone else a page-folder like me? Trust me, you will be coming back to it time and time again, just like I do. Enjoy!

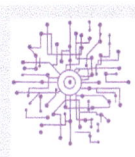

CURIOSITY = + ENGAGEMENT

When we can add an element of curiosity, we increase engagement levels.

HEADLINES TO REMEMBER FOR THE ENGAGEMENT STORE CUPBOARD

- Curiosity is a key element in engagement
- Curiosity can be found throughout this book
- Humble resources can be the missing element to engagement!

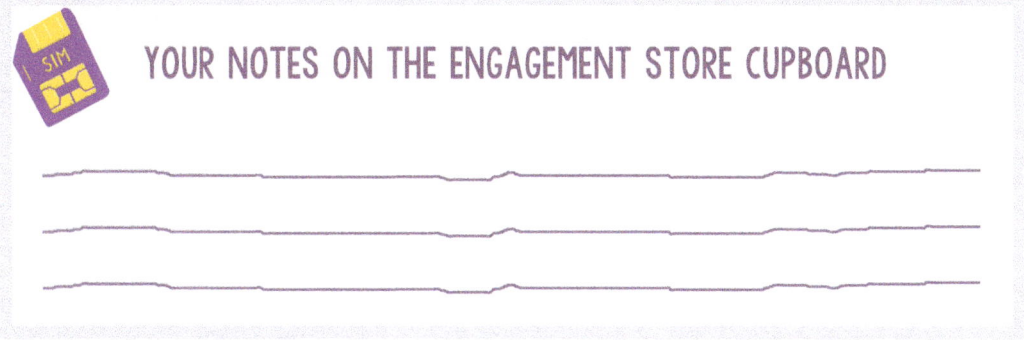

YOUR NOTES ON THE ENGAGEMENT STORE CUPBOARD

CHAPTER 7

Neuroaffirming essentials interview

'The behaviour policy works for everyone except SEND students.'

This was the 'good news' a deputy head was delivering on a training day. I heard it like a sack of sand hitting the floor. How? How can this be good news? How can this be a triumph? It is actually one of the reasons I felt compelled to write this book. Because engagement unlocks a love of learning. All children deserve to love learning. All children deserve to succeed. If it isn't working for SEND students, it isn't working. We can do better. And we will. By learning new strategies together.

The DfE released full data on SEND in schools taken from the January census (DfE, 2024). The headline data showed:

- a total of 18.4 per cent of children in England have some kind of special educational need – up from 17.3 per cent in 2023;
- that's a total of 1,673,205 children with SEND, which is an increase of over **100,000 from 2023**;
- there's been a 7.1 per cent increase in the number of children on SEN support who have no noted type of assessed need;
- speech, language and communication needs remain the most common type of need for SEN support, with autism being the highest type of need for those with an EHCP.

Time and time again we are confusing disengagement or undesirable behaviour with blocked access. This issue is becoming increasingly more prevalent in schools. If we want our children to engage in the learning, we have to ensure every child has an all-access pass to the lesson.

If you feel like you can't get through your lesson because of needs, this section is going to be a firm favourite for you. The problem is SEND training is so sparse and inconsistent.

Teachers are not equipped around what 'neuroaffirming' actually means, let alone what it might look like in our class. Often it conjures up nightmares of creating 30 different lesson plans. But actually, neuroaffirming strategies save us time, not take it away! It is all about simple tweaks and adaptations that support all children to thrive.

I was lucky enough to sit down with my very good friend and talented colleague, Tanyel Salih. The author of *The Adaptive Teaching Planner* (2025) and advisory teacher, Tan also works within The Good Morning Club (TGMC) as our TGMC SENCO and a TGMC trainer. We unpick what challenges educators are facing in the classroom and simple tools that all teachers can use to ensure each child has every opportunity to thrive in our lessons.

In your magical manual I have shared my top ten neuroaffirming strategies and solutions that can be used in (almost) every lesson. In this interview I unpick these further with Tan.

Before we start, shall we just address the elephant in the room? What in fresh hell do we mean by 'neuroaffirming strategies'?

Neuroaffirming strategies are about accepting and embracing that all learners think differently. It is about teaching in a way that all types of learners can benefit from – as opposed to teaching to neurotypical learners and having everyone else play catch-up. Neuroaffirming strategies ensure children don't feel 'othered' and instead understand their strengths and value difference.

If you're anything like me, this may be fairly new. I wasn't taught about neuroaffirming strategies. I read about it. I had no idea I was eliminating learners with certain strategies; I was just doing my best with the information I had. Let's delve in!

INTERVIEW WITH TANYEL SALIH

Tan, tell me, what typical strategies are happening in classrooms all over the world right now that create hurdles for our neurodivergent children?

Presenting children with too much information both visually and verbally. I totally understand that as an educator there is SO much to get through and the curriculum moves really fast. But, ultimately, it is in our best interest to provide opportunities to pace and chunk learning. Not only will this support children to access the task, it will also support their wellbeing and relationship with school. Often our biggest hurdle is our assumptions. We might assume because children are of a certain age they can do certain things. But there are so many factors involved from how children retain information to environmental factors and even down to the type of morning they have had. It is so important to remove those assumptions to ensure all children can thrive in that lesson.

What is one of the biggest misconceptions you see from educators when it comes to neuroaffirming strategies?

That they are only for certain students at certain times. Neuroaffirming strategies can be practised and accessed by all students at any time. A great example of this is when *we visited HSV international school. In their classrooms they had headphones. When talking to one of the pupils, I asked what they were for. She said, sometimes we might want or need quiet, for example if we are writing. She shared that the class can freely get headphones when needed. This is a great example of any child having access to support their learning and wellbeing.

Tan and I worked with HSV international school in The Hague for TGMC training and consultation.

What does 'adaptive teaching' actually mean and how does it align with neuroaffirming strategies?

Adaptive teaching is about knowing the starting point of your class. Every class will have different needs, whether it is SEND, family dynamics, ACEs or something else that impacts their starting point. Adaptive teaching is about responding to the needs of the pupils and meeting them where they are. We will be able to do this through the types of questions we ask and ways in which children can respond, in order to do that we need to have conversations with their previous teachers, professionals and their families. We need to stay up to date with the latest research and above all we need to ask questions about what our children might need and stay curious. Neuroaffirming strategies are the tools and prompts that help you to adapt.

Let's talk about some of our practical strategies for educators. Why are timers such a staple in the classroom?

There are a variety of ways to use timers and a variety of different timers. It is important to note that not all timers might be helpful for all children. For example, some children may find digital timers or loud timers anxiety-inducing. There are so many options though like sand timers, dial timers or silent Canva timers. Timers support you to establish clear and achievable expectations, especially for children who struggle to understand or follow time concepts such as 'Five more minutes left'. Timers make this tangible. Sometimes a task might feel overwhelming, and it can be unclear where to start. Timers support children to approach through micro steps. It is also important to note the long-term impact of implementing timers as a strategy. When children move to secondary school, they need to be able to organise themselves and these skills lay the foundation for that.

There are lots of misconceptions about fidgets. As you know, I am a huge fan. What would you say to an educator who was concerned about fidgets being used for novelty in the classroom?

I think what is key is the WHY. Why have we introduced them? It is important to involve children in that journey. We know the neuroaffirming essentials are research backed, we know they work. But we need to provide that story for children to build a schema of understanding around something that might feel fairly new. Explicitly, teaching this supports pupils' metacognition and self-awareness. It is also important, as with teaching anything new, to set the expectations and boundaries. It is important to do this in a collaborative way as we would with any expectations.

Most educators will have heard of a *now* and *next*, but can you explain from your expertise why these are so valuable?

Imagine a pupil who has low self-esteem about their learning. They have arrived at school and are unsure what is happening. There is an English book on their table and a learning intention has been shared. They have no idea where to start. Using a *now*, *next* and *then* (or *first*, *second*, *third*) lightens the load.

For example, the first part might be reading the paragraph. We then might encourage children to highlight the verbs and, finally, write a sentence with one of the verbs.

Now, children can prioritise and are clear on how to achieve. What is really important is not making this an isolated strategy. Put it on the board to help all children and support that seamless start to tasks.

Of course, it is great to have handy extras in the classroom, but make it a whole-class neuroaffirming strategy when you can.

What do you think is the biggest barrier to adaptive teaching and how can we overcome it?

Assuming that it needs to be extra or additional, when we work together and when we use neuroaffirming essentials, it builds fluency and has a positive impact on a child's relationship with school. It isn't an extra teach, it is a shift in how we teach and how children are invited to respond and be a part of the learning. It is so important to remember you are not alone and to start small! Look at the neuroaffirming essentials and start with one thing at a time.

From your extensive experience, which school strategy or resource have you seen to be most impactful for children?

Multisensory teaching and learning opportunities. This could be tangible items, visuals or videos.

We want our students to be fully invited into the lesson. Making learning tangible and bringing it to life will support them with their comprehension, language development and accessibility of the task.

What would you say to the educator who is feeling unsure about neuroaffirming strategies?

You are not alone. Remember to be the biggest advocate for your children and lean on the support around you. Just as we know small steps are impactful for our children, they are also impactful for you. Don't overwhelm yourself. Start with one step at a time. Use your neuroaffirming essentials as a starting point for this. You've got this!

Exercise actually changes the brain's anatomy, physiology and function.

Dr Wendy Suzuki

M is for movement

'I just wonder if an inspector came in, would they be able to see the children are learning?'

'But they are so ...'

'No, I understand, but there is a lot of movement. It looks a bit chaotic.'

That was the 'conversation' I had with one of my senior leaders in my first year of teaching. I was super-excited to trial an escape room-style maths lesson. Children were working in groups solving problems, a range of manipulatives were sprawled across tables, children were leaning over, standing up, working on the floor and walking across the maths displays for clues. The room was buzzing. I was told to shut it down.

Keep them in chairs. Move as little as possible. Stick to worksheets. This conveyer belt teaching was the expectation.

In my sixth year of teaching, I moved to Malaysia to teach abroad. I had five years of KS2 (ages seven to 11) under my belt, but found myself thrown into a mixed Reception/Year 1 class (ages four to six). English was their third language (how impressive is that by the way?). I *struggled*. The conveyer belt approach I had lived by was not an option. They didn't want to sit. The worksheet model was completely pointless. And I felt like I was learning to teach all over again. So what if I didn't read *The Three Little Pigs* 12 times in a row and just hope for the best? It was time to colour outside the lines.

What if, as I read it, we acted it out together? What if we played a PE game where they ran to the houses? What if we used dance and yoga storytelling? What if we actually built the houses? Felt the materials? What if we focused on **doing** more?

That might seem so obvious to read. But for 2017 Jen, that was a walk on the wild side. Turns out, static learning isn't actually the best route for learning. Static learning is like asking everyone to go sailing in a pedalo. Why create obstacles before you begin?

LEARNING POSITIONS

Look at these images. Which child is learning best?

1.   **2.**   **3.**

Figure 8.1   Learning positions

We might have said sitting cross legged, because that is how we have been forced to sit. You might have been told by an observer that your children aren't learning because they are not sitting in a uniform way. There are many notions such as 'whole-body listening', 'SLANT' and 'STAR' sitting that your setting might promote and look for. You may have a reward system or sanction system that praises stillness. Or you might have jumped straight to the rock climbing because we can connect that to our own experiences of learning. The truth is each of them could show learning. But our educational system has agreed on a chosen *look* and message: sitting in a uniform way is the best way to learn. Right? Wrong … **Our brain and body work together like an ecosystem.**

WAIT, BACK UP A SECOND. HOW DID WE GET TO A SYSTEM THAT VALUES STILLNESS?

If you're anything like me, you might be thinking, but, we *have* always done it this way. There must be a reason we came to the conclusion that static learning wins the Game of Thrones …

Our formal education system can be traced back to Prussia. Shall we take a lil' history tour together? I'll make it short. Basically, Prussia (now part of Russia) was having a real problem creating loyal soldiers. The soldiers they were recruiting didn't really care.

They didn't want any part of it; their life was at the farm. So, what if they added some threats? A death penalty for soldiers not standing their ground. Well, they didn't respect that either and revolted. So, what if we create a new generation of loyal soldiers who respect authority and uniform? It will start with an institution of authority and formalisation. School.

We can also look at the Victorian Era in Britain as the real push for funded formal schooling in Great Britain. Both of these systems have many things in common, but one that stands out is the factory approach. Let's get them schooled in the most resourceful and efficient way possible. Having children sit still just makes sense. It wasn't about providing the best possible education for our children. It was about creating workers as quickly as possible. We can see how sitting children down was viewed as the best option here.

Figure 8.2   1975 comic on the factory model of education (Explore-Blog, 2013)

Hard to believe this cartoon was created in 1975, right?

So, what do we need to know about movement and its role in learning? Is it really all that great?

LET'S START WITH EMBODIED COGNITION ...

'WE ARE NOT BRAINS ON STICKS' (WELL DAMN)

The theoretical framework of embodied cognition basically tells us in order to learn better and more deeply, we must recognise that our cognitive processes are deeply intertwined with our bodily interactions. Basically, to get the brain to RSVP to learning we need to invite the body too.

MOVEMENT INCREASES BLOOD FLOW TO THE BRAIN

Ooh, sounds fancy right? What do we really mean by this? Well, blood flow to the brain is like petrol for a car. When blood flows to the brain it carries essential food like glucose and oxygen which makes our brains love life. It improves attention, focus, memory and mood. It is essential to learning and cognitive function. Did you know that Steve Jobs used to have 'walking meetings' instead of the traditional 'sit down and try and stay awake meetings'. He knew we think better when we are moving. A team of researchers at Stanford conducted a study to delve into this connection Radhakrishnan (2023). They divided participants into two groups: one walked on a treadmill and the other remained seated. Both groups were then tasked with creative thinking exercises. Spoiler alert, but the group that walked on the treadmill demonstrated a significant boost in creative thinking compared to the seated group which continued after the walking had occurred. We like! What else?

MOVEMENT STRENGTHENS NEURONS AND HELPS TO BUILD NEW ONES

Research has uncovered that exercise and movement impacts BDNF levels, which stands for *brain-derived neurotrophic factor*. Lots of big words, but what do they mean? BDNF is like fertiliser for neurons. So, movement actually impacts brain plasticity (and mood). In particular, neuroscientists are sharing how exercise can stimulate new generations of neurons in the hippocampus. This is the region of the brain associated with memory.

MOVEMENT RELEASES HAPPY HORMONES IN OUR BODY

Our happy hormones love movement! We can actually tick off each one through different kinds of movement. Endorphins are released through energetic movements, serotonin is released through any movement outside, oxytocin is released when we move in groups like dances, yoga or group actions. Dopamine is released when we set goals through movement. Happy hormones kind of do what they say on the tin. They make us feel better. When we feel better we do better. So, doesn't it just make sense to integrate movement in as many ways as possible?

SITTING IS THE NEW SMOKING

There is increasingly more research about our reliance on sitting. Within the last five years or so we have seen the rise of the standing desk and even some treadmill desks (I'm jealous to be honest!). But is this a trend or something to be taken seriously? Well, the science shows us that standing up more supports our alertness, focus and overall active engagement. Finland is often considered one of the best education systems in the world. Did you know they have a 15-minute outdoor break every 45 minutes of learning? Really puts my ten-hour library sessions writing my dissertation in perspective!

100 PER CENT OF TEACHERS IN MY COMMUNITY FEEL THAT THE CURRICULUM IS OVERCROWDED

Here's the thing, we are often closing one book to open the next. There is a wealth of research for both concentrated work and short bursts. Concentrated work allows us to immerse ourselves in 'flow' and deep thinking. Whereas short bursts keep us focused and alert. However, it seems that our curriculum doesn't quite achieve either. Just as children are delving into Roman battlefields, we have to flip the switch to improper fractions.

How does this have anything to do with movement? Well, if we were deep in flow we might find ourselves exploring on the floor or changing positions. If we were in short bursts our body would be up and about getting oxygen to the brain. But we tend to miss both trains, leaving children static and disengaged.

SITTING STILL

I don't know about you. But sometimes when I read research it can fly over my head. To process it better, I like to think about it personally. I also like to think about the opposite of what the research highlights. So, let's think about a time we were sitting still for a prolonged period of time. For me, driving lessons come to mind. My instructor kept saying rule after rule and all I could think was DON'T CRASH. I couldn't compute anything else. Sitting still makes you tired. Isn't that the weirdest correlation? Afterwards my mood was rock bottom, and my brain felt super-foggy.

TAKE A MOMENT TO THINK ABOUT THE LAST TIME YOU WERE STILL FOR TOO LONG

I'm not talking about laying by the pool here, I am talking about a learning situation.

- When was the last time you sat still learning?
- How did you feel?
- How did it impact your learning?
- What would you do differently in future?

IS THE ANSWER MOVEMENT BREAKS?

This is a standard and well-intentioned practice in many schools. But it kind of misses the point. If we know our brains and bodies work as an ecosystem, isolating movement and learning into separate activities throughout the day doesn't really make sense. Yes, there may be times when we need an extra wriggle or a routine movement. But as a whole, we should be looking at integrating movement into as much of the school day as possible. This doesn't mean translating the curriculum into an interpretive dance! As you will discover in PART 2, this can be achieved in a variety of ways throughout the day.

WON'T IT MAKE CHILDREN MORE EXCITED?

Such a valid concern! This is about exploring the type of movement you are employing with your class. Not all movement is high-energy cardio. Movement is about involving our body in learning. Regulation has a big role to play in what movement tasks we use. For example, after lunch it would be more beneficial to do floor work or multisensory tasks like play-dough rather than going straight into a scavenger hunt. This provides appropriate stimulation. If we use a high-energy movement task when children feel tired, we can risk a sensory overload causing something we have all experienced as 'the giggles!' We will explore more about regulation in Chapter 13.

ISN'T IT HARDER TO MANAGE?

I didn't want to integrate movement for this very reason. Once they're up and about, how do I manage that? How do I remain in control? Do I need to remain in control? What will it look like? It is all about setting up for success and we are going to delve into the logistics in PART 2.

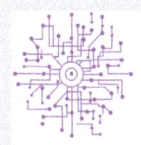

MOVEMENT = + THINKING + OVERALL HAPPINESS

Children who can think better and feel better are going to naturally be more engaged.

HEADLINES TO REMEMBER FOR MOVEMENT IN THE CLASSROOM

- We need to stop valuing stillness
- There is a wealth of research pointing towards more movement
- Movement doesn't necessarily mean a group workout

YOUR NOTES ON THE ENGAGEMENT STORE CUPBOARD

Nearly always, in an unstructured class exchange, a few students do most of the shared thinking, talking and practising. It's not a good way to run a room if you want everyone thinking.

Tom Sherrington (2022)

CHAPTER 9

A is for: a task not an ask

'Same hands again, anyone else? Come on team!'

Every time I said it, I wanted to shake myself. *Stop saying that, it doesn't work.* But my frustration spoke before my logic. My lesson would be going great up until the point I asked a question. Then I would feel the climate change. Heads would drop, hands would wander, a blanket of muttering would cover the room, and the same three to five children would wave their hands frantically. Then, two things happened.

The child I picked would have such a well-intentioned beautiful answer. But not quite the right one. It would drag on; I would want to acknowledge and recognise them, but also ensure the correct answer was heard by all children. We've all been in that situation (don't leave me hanging now) where we turn on the paraphrase '... I think what you mean is ...', trying to salvage the direction of the lesson while not crushing the self-esteem of the child!

The alternative was I picked a child, they gave me the model answer and I felt great about myself. CRUSHING this lesson. But when children started the task, or I marked books, I could see my formative assessment was pretty inaccurate.

So, hands up wasn't helping me and it wasn't engaging my kids. But a life without hands up? Forget about it. It was a classroom staple. I wasn't sure how I would possibly manage a class without it. During that year (this was my sixth year of teaching) I was approached to join a research group. Now, this was very exciting for me. I freaking love research. It was about trialling the 'Teach like a Champion' principles in a range of classes across the school. This was a school that went from age four to 18. At the time I was working with a mixed Reception/Year 1 class.

My rule was 'no opt out.' Which meant if you ask a question, everyone should be able to answer it, and you should practise cold calling and supportive techniques to achieve this. This was the beginning of my journey, but I will be honest. It felt more about rigorous high expectations rather than engagement. The last thing I ever want is for the children in my class to be scared. We know safety is essential to children thriving. Cold calling wasn't giving safety for me. A few years later, *task don't ask* replaced hands up.

The concept of task don't ask is switching a question with a whole-class task. This means, ALL children are invited which will **drastically increase participation, engagement and overall focus**. It also moves away from right/wrong, which can deter children, and provides more intrigue!

WAIT WHAT?

Let me show you some examples:

If the ask is ...	A task could be ...
What did a Roman soldier's meal consist of?	Draw a Roman soldier's meal on your whiteboard
Do you think this character is a good friend?	The character is a good friend. Stand up if you agree, sit down if you don't
Which noun is abstract?	(Number the nouns) Show me with your fingers, which noun is abstract?

Shift   LET'S THINK

When we ask a question ...	👍	👎
Do all kids put their hands up?	○	○
Do the same kids put their hands up?	○	○
Does it impact the pace of your lesson?	○	○
Do you ever have children that talk too long?	○	○
Do you ever have to paraphrase to get to the right answer?	○	○
Do some children zone out?	○	○
Do some children still not get it when they start the task?	○	○

And what about you? Picture living your best staff meeting life (it happens!) and the person leading says: 'Does anyone have any questions?' Picture the room, feel the vibe.

Same situation, but this time the person leading says:

'I have spoken a lot. Here are the main points I covered in this staff meeting on this slide. Have a read through to yourself. I am going to hand everyone a sticky note, write a question or thought from the session.'

Picture the room. Feel the vibe. It's switched right? Suddenly, it doesn't feel like you have a microphone, it feels connected, calm and purposeful. Why? This quote sheds more light on that feeling.

Enforcing the 'hands up' rule will result in a proportion of learners feeling alienated; after all, if only the learners who put their hands up are actively involved within the lesson, then the participation and interest of others swiftly diminishes. And if you are a student that actively wants to disengage, then the 'hands up' rule is ideal.

Lewis (2015)

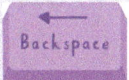

WAIT, BACK UP A SECOND. WHERE DID 'HANDS UP' COME FROM?

I was in a Reception class recently. A child's whiteboard pen ran out in her phonics lesson. She purposefully got up and walked to collect one. With a pen in her hand, she turned to go back to her carpet space, but before she got there a teacher intervened. 'You need to put your hand up and ask for a pen.' She said it calmly and kindly, but, nonetheless, took the pen and the child walked back to her spot where she subsequently raised her hand.

I can't tell you how many times I have said: 'Hands up to answer a question' or 'Hands up to speak/get out of your seat' etc. I GET IT. Believe me. From a management perspective we think it would be Lord of the Flies if we took away this signal. But when you look at that example above, it feels like (in some cases) hands up creates an unnecessary barrier for engagement.

(Continued)

There are so many amazing pedagogical approaches to questioning. I am a Bloom's Taxonomy fan myself! But great questions and hands up don't necessarily go hand in hand. We often find ourselves asking questions when we have the terrifying realisation we have spoken for way too long and actually need some water! When I was training to be a teacher, I used to print out my PowerPoint Slides and write three questions next to each slide. THREE. I had about 75 slides back then. Coincidentally, I thought this would improve my engagement and not deter it.

The truth is, it was a foundational non-negotiable classroom strategy. It is what I saw all my mentors do. It's what we did. Many of us (understandably) still do.

I always think it's worth taking a trip down memory lane when it comes to legacy strategies to think about our own experiences and thoughts with it. It's a great opportunity to look at it critically!

TAKE A MOMENT TO JOURNEY BACK

- What were your initial experiences with 'hands up to answer the question'?
- Have you ever doubted it or felt like it hindered engagement?
- Where do you stand now?

NO OPT OUT: THE ESSENCE IS STILL THERE

The foundational principle of no opt out is there. The basic idea is that we aren't relying on a handful of students to navigate the lesson and control the pace. However, the supporting argument of no opt out emphasises more on control rather than engagement. It talks about children saying 'I don't know' as a 'cop out' and some articles refer to children as lazy (Lemov, 2010). This isn't about cracking the whip. We want children to want to learn, not be cornered into it.

NOT PASSIVE, NOT SCARED

Here's the thing: on the one hand, when we routinely and consistently ask questions, we create a sense of opt out. This encourages passive learners which is a stone's throw away from (dare I say it?) boredom. On the other hand, cold calling is more likely to increase vigilance, rather than engagement. None of us go into our classrooms with the goal of scaring children. I know that for certain if you're reading this book. Tasking removes that anxiety. Tasking is all about involvement THAT is what we want to achieve in our lessons.

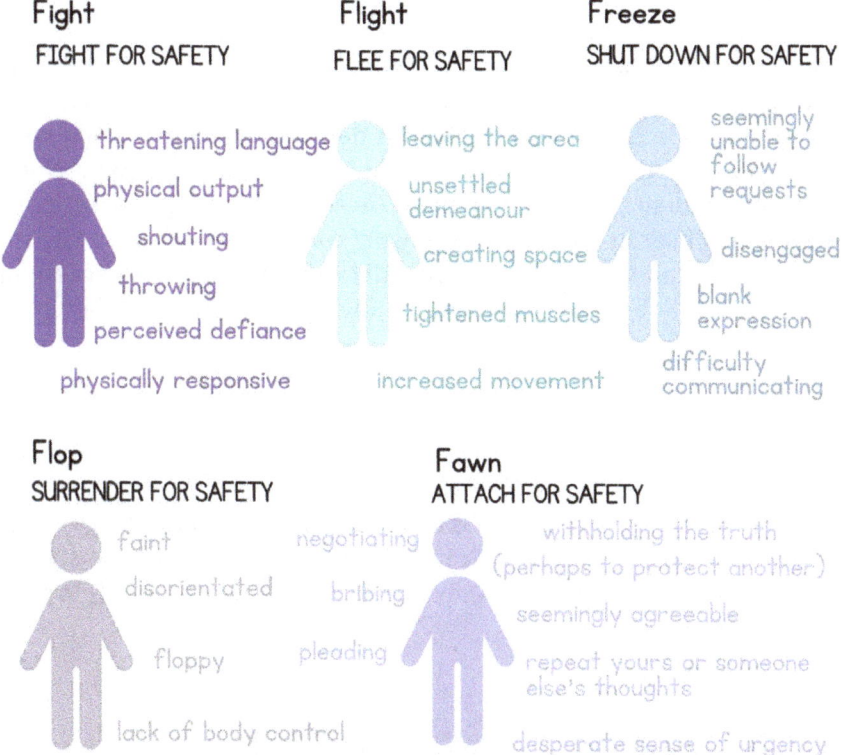

Fight
FIGHT FOR SAFETY

threatening language

physical output

shouting

throwing

perceived defiance

physically responsive

Flight
FLEE FOR SAFETY

leaving the area

unsettled demeanour

creating space

tightened muscles

increased movement

Freeze
SHUT DOWN FOR SAFETY

seemingly unable to follow requests

disengaged

blank expression

difficulty communicating

Flop
SURRENDER FOR SAFETY

faint

disorientated

floppy

lack of body control

negotiating

bribing

pleading

Fawn
ATTACH FOR SAFETY

withholding the truth (perhaps to protect another)

seemingly agreeable

repeat yours or someone else's thoughts

desperate sense of urgency

Figure 9.1   What we might see in the classroom if children feel scared

SOCIAL CONTAGION

Social contagion is the concept that behaviours and ideas spread like a virus. It sounds a bit icky, but it is actually a super-powerful phenomenon to tap into in the classroom (Barrett, 2021). The basic rule is, we are more likely to get involved if our pals are. Honestly, this happened to me at lunch the other day. I wasn't sure whether to order a small plate or a big plate. My two friends ordered a big plate which made my decision easy! If we enter a quiet place like a library we immediately lower our voices. And if there's a conga at a wedding it would be much weirder to **not** join in. So, when we ask a question, we are removing that social contagion effect. Children know not everyone can be chosen and therefore don't feel the instinctual need to want to put their hand up as the odds are against them. But a task?

Everyone is doing the task. Seeing everyone doing a task knee jerks you to join in too! And it feels good to be **a part of** something rather than competing for it.

WAIT TIME AND PROCESSING

On average, we wait less than a second after asking a question. If a child does not respond during this time, we often repeat the question, rephrase it, or give our own answer (Busch, 2024). Why? Because the curriculum is demanding, crowded and we are often thinking more about getting **through** the lesson rather than being **in** it. When we task instead of ask, we naturally provide more time. We aren't expecting a racket ball response. It's a task after all. Children have time to actually complete it. Research has shown that increasing wait time can lead to more thoughtful and complete answers and increased student engagement (Sobel and Alston, 2021). This also lends itself to better processing and deeper learning.

BUZZ OVER DUD

When all children are doing a task there is definite buzz and focus in the classroom. When we are taking turns picking children with their hands up it feels like time stands still. The energy is zapped from the room and one by one children find *other* things to engage them instead.

FORMATIVE ASSESSMENT

We cannot gauge how well children have understood the learning by two or three contributions from the class. But when 100 per cent of children are invited to do a task, well, that's just good odds! During that task we are able to get a whole-class snapshot, supporting us to intervene and direct the lesson effectively.

TASK DON'T ASK CONVERTS

I asked some of my community how task don't ask impacted their engagement and this is what they said:

> Task don't ask is the best thing I have done this year. It is so much fun and my children are so much more engaged. It has been particularly helpful for my 'reluctant sharers'.
>
> Alison, class teacher in Edinburgh

Word wave has been amazing in particular. It really helped increase the confidence and participation of my learners.

Rosie, teacher trainee in Hertfordshire

I am now able to formatively assess EAL children who can be afraid of speaking up and they are actually engaged!

Corinna, class teacher in London

Instead of asking the meaning of words in English, I tasked children to draw them. EVERY child had a go and were having lovely, meaningful conversations with each other.

Molly, class teacher in Southampton

Task don't ask has been an absolute game changer for me! I'm so glad I found TGMC at the beginning of my teaching career!

Melanie, early career teacher (ECT)

From my greater depth children to SEND, every child has been engaged and can access the learning consistently with 'task don't ask'. It has made a difference in every subject!

Kelly, deputy head in Wiltshire

The children used to get so bored waiting for me to finish my teacher input before they could get stuck in. But now they are all involved and joining in!

Victoria, class teacher in Essex

LET'S UNPICK SOME POSSIBLE BARRIERS ...

WHAT IF CHILDREN WANT TO ASK A QUESTION?

Of course! The last thing we want to do is muzzle our kids. This is where non-verbal signals come in handy. It is like an additional conversation that can happen at all times without disruption. Read about it in the magical manual! GOLD.

(Continued)

CAN I NEVER ASK A HANDS UP QUESTION?

Let's be clear. We aren't reprimanding a hand in the air. This isn't a 'no hands up' policy. This is about replacing your 'asks' with a 'task' to improve engagement. Where appropriate. There will be times where hands up just makes sense. For example:

- hands up if you walked to school today
- hands up if you'd like to volunteer.

We don't want to criminalise hands up, we want to level up engagement. When we start looking critically at the hands up culture we realise there are many better and effective alternatives. For example, non-verbal signals to go to the toilet or get a drink support the flow of your lesson much better than children putting their hand up and asking.

WHAT IF IT REQUIRES MORE OF AN ANSWER THAN A QUICK TASK?

Got a meaty question that feels like more than a quick task? Maybe it requires more inference or explanation. Totally get it. But if we do hands up, we can't hear everyone's answer. We also need to consider that if it is a meaty one, it is going to take longer to answer, which is harder for children to sustain focus. In this situation, it might be more about breaking it up into different tasks that lean into conversation and collaboration. For example, a partner talk, or a group debate.

I DON'T HAVE TIME TO DO A TASK EVERY TIME I WANT TO ASK A QUESTION

When I started tasking instead of asking it really made me examine the volume of questions I was asking before. It would go something like 'This week we have been looking at a new book; who remembers the title? Yes, *Ruby's Worry*! What happened to Ruby's worry in the book, who can tell me? You're right it got bigger! So, what was it that helped the worry get smaller? Hands up if you remember.'

I honestly asked a question every couple of sentences. Most of which were totally unnecessary and slowed my engagement. If we look at it face on paper, it would definitely be pretty cumbersome to do a task for each of those questions and we would never get anything done. But what is the main question there? We are reviewing the text. So, instead of asking a series of questions, we could share a picture of the book and ask our class to talk to their partner about everything they can remember. We could even share those questions on the board and gradually reveal them throughout the partner talk. Alternatively, we could ask children to draw everything they remember from the story on their whiteboard or even storyboard it. This supports ALL children to participate and ALL children to stay on task.

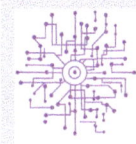

$$\frac{\text{TASK}}{\text{ASK}} = + \text{ENGAGEMENT}$$

Giving a task supports 100 per cent engagement.

HEADLINES TO REMEMBER ON TASKS

- Tasking supports 100 per cent participation
- Tasking supports the pace of your lesson
- Tasking supports the energy of your lesson

YOUR NOTES ON TASKS

Note down three things you want to remember from this chapter and take forward into your teaching and classroom.

_____

_____

_____

_____

_____

_____

_____

School is dull. There I said it. We need to think.
What is it that we are trying to do here, and if we have to do it, is there
another way?

Greg Bottrill (2022)

G is for game time

CHAPTER 10

'If you're going to do anything at home with your child, make it a game.'

Have you ever said that to parents or guardians? Has it ever been direct advice to you? I've been on both sides of that statement. Desperately trying to convince families that a tutor or a workbook isn't the missing ingredient for your child to love school. But games, games will bring learning together in a new concoction. I was recently on the other side of that statement. I sat in my first parent meeting at Miles' school. Taking notes, obvs. The headteacher led a session on maths and urged us, don't overthink maths at home. Play snakes and ladders. I smiled. Think about how many skills are learnt through snakes and ladders. You've got turn-taking which, to be honest, was the hardest with Miles! Maths-wise we've got subitising, counting, sequencing, pattern recognition, place value and all of this was achieved without a single flashcard. The best thing with games is: children **want** to do it again and again. Consolidating those skills with ease.

We know the power of play. But play gets put into a weird filing cabinet. We encourage, love and respect the power of play in the Early Years, but then it seems to get filed away as deemed unnecessary as soon as children turn six.

We know that 70 per cent of children play video games. We can visibly see how prevalent gaming is in our society. Some of us can barely get through a day without hearing a reference to Minecraft® or Roblox® (Fábrega, 2023).

But I'm actually not talking solely about either of these concepts. Don't get me wrong, these are great topics and there are many books that delve deeply into both of them. And of course, they tap into engagement.

But this book is about the unwritten code of engagement. This book is about everyday practice across every year group. What if we could lean into play *and* gaming? In this chapter I want to talk about playful games. There's play and there's playful. Playful is the intention of your approach. Playful is a twist on the tradition. I think we can tap into **playful games** every lesson.

WAIT, WHAT IS A PLAYFUL GAME?

When I am referring to playful games, I mean any type of game or playful activity linked to your learning. It can be board games, word games, whiteboard games, active games … we will explore them all in the magic manual section! But think: GAMES.

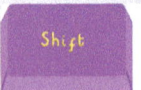

Shift   WHICH ACTIVITY?

I am going to give you two scenarios; use a pen to tick or cross off on the following questions.

It's the first day of a new school year. You're planning your activities. Which activity below would you give the boot? Cross out the one that doesn't make the cut.

- Two truths and a lie
- Parachute games
- Ordering events of the summer
- Making chatterboxes/fortune tellers

Let's shift to staff training. Which activity below would you give the boot?

- Read and answer questions about cognitive load
- Work in teams, have a bucket in each team and add thoughts in the bucket to show cognitive load of a child throughout the day
- Play **Which one doesn't belong?** with a list of words associated with cognitive load

Look at the activities you crossed out and the activities you left. Sure, I could have spoken about the importance of playful games in learning. That is en route! But you've kind of done that yourself right? Your own instincts speak pretty loudly. It is likely you opted for the more playful options.

We can also unpick how your attention may have changed while reading that. You were asked to partake in … a game. Albeit not the most thrilling of games. But did it pique your focus? Did you grab a pen? Did you think more deeply?

We are naturally drawn to playful games. As George Bernard Shaw said, **'We don't stop playing because we grow old; we grow old because we stop playing.'**

There's a reason we automatically search for 'icebreakers' in the first week of school. It's because we know playing games diffuses anxiety. We know games support 100 per cent participation and we know we are more likely to cultivate some laughs with our class through games rather than formal learning.

While games may not be strictly *necessary* for survival in modern society, they tap into deep-rooted human instincts and provide a valuable outlet for exploration, social interaction and cognitive development (Dearybury and Jones, 2020).

We have all experienced setting the class off on task to be met with … the resistance. Think about the resistance that some children present when it's time to pick up a pen. Think about that resistance to start *the work*. We don't experience that with games. We often experience 'the buzz'. The desperation to start rather than the string of reasons they cannot.

Playful games can be used to replace some of those more traditional lesson elements like worksheets, where we often meet 'the resistance'.

WAIT, BACK UP A SECOND. PLAYFUL GAMES AREN'T ANYTHING NEW

As an educator, think of any historical topic you have taught. I bet you had a lesson about the games that time period played! Dice games can be traced back to Ancient Egyptians. Ball games to the Ancient Mayans and card games to the Tang Dynasty. We see games in every culture and throughout history. Where we are facing a disconnect is bringing that into the classroom – not as a 'treat', but as a respected pedagogical approach.

We don't have a handy timeline of where this has all gone wrong. But we have to look at the overall culture of the education system. Let me shed some personal insight based on my experiences within the profession and working with thousands of teachers. **Book look** … ring a bell?

When I started teaching 13 years ago, book scrutiny was regular and thorough. I would also like to add … brutal. If you haven't been exposed to this, a book scrutiny is when someone goes through a selection (if not all) of your children's books to see the learning process.

I have worked in a number of schools, and it is always a similar message. 'Prove to me you have taught a high-quality lesson every day.' Now depending on your setting these will be varying degrees of pointless and damaging. Hopefully, you have had better experiences than I have. But regardless, this attitude to learning evokes two key issues:

- we communicate that written evidence is more valuable, pushing games to the sideline;
- we communicate a lack of trust in pedagogy to our teachers, bringing the textbook to the forefront.

Of course, these practices always start with the best of intentions for our children. But it's time to remove barriers and put playful games back on the lesson plan.

WHY PLAYFUL GAMES DESERVE A REGULAR SLOT IN YOUR LESSONS

YOUR HAPPY HORMONES LOVE PLAYFUL GAMES

Happy hormones are a group of neurotransmitters that play a crucial role in regulating mood, emotions and wellbeing. These hormones are released in response to positive experiences and can contribute to feelings of happiness, joy and contentment. Our happy hormones love games!

Dopamine is our reward chemical. It is released in response to rewards, achievements and positive experiences within a game. When children 'win' a game or feel a sense of progress the brain releases dopamine which increases our motivation. It also explains why children often ask to play 'just one more time!'

Serotonin is associated with mood regulation and often plays a role in that enjoyment of playing a game. I mean, when was the last time you played a game and didn't feel just a little bit giddier?

Our friend oxytocin also comes out to play during game time. Pun intended. Oxytocin is known as the love chemical. When we play games with others, we feel a sense of connection and community. Not only is this crucial to our engagement, but also to our overall wellbeing.

YOUR BRAIN LOVES PLAYFUL GAMES

When we play games, we increase neuroplasticity which allows the brain to learn and grow (Brown and Vaughan, 2010). We like!

Play also stimulates the growth of neural connections and strengthens current networks. Basically, better learning and better remembering! We will always be more likely to remember a game rather than a worksheet. This is because when we play we are encoding information and our memory is strengthened. This happens because we are having fun and are actively involved.

When we are playing games, we are immersed from a sensory perspective which means we are far more likely to stay engaged.

PLAYFUL GAMES INCORPORATE GROWTH MINDSET

Who remembers Snake? If you don't, oh my goodness please search **Nokia 3310 Snake** immediately and live your best life.

Did you play once and put it down? Of course not, you wanted to get better, and you weren't too fussed by the setbacks. It didn't feel like there were two categories of winner or loser. It felt like there was the choice to pursue and get better or not. Isn't this what we want our children to feel every lesson?

This growth mindset energy is a big win with games. The pressure is lifted, you don't have to do it in a handwriting pen. And when you get it wrong it doesn't feel like the same type of wrong. It just feels like part of the journey. Playful games are amazing at encouraging resilience with ease.

PLAYFUL GAMES ENHANCE COMMUNITY

I once had a child who would seemingly sabotage his partner's work. He would scribble on it, rip it up and when addressed he would feel so embarrassed. I'm not going to lie; it was a struggle to identify what was happening and it was frustrating. One day he said, 'Her writing is so much neater.'

I'm sharing this because so much of what we do naturally in school is a comparison game. Once again, this is a catalyst for 'the resistance'. Children don't want to partake if they feel like they are going to be measured. Especially children who are more self-aware and understand what areas they find trickier.

What is so special about playful games is that children are working and playing together. This supports community over competition. Which is a much stronger force for engagement. Because when children (and adults) feel like they belong and are a part of something, they want to be involved. We will delve more into this within Chapter 12, C is for connect (Barrett, 2021).

PLAY AND FLOW

One of my favourite theories from Mihaly Csikszentmihalyi (1975) is the theory of flow. This refers to a psychological state where time falls away and we are completely immersed in what we are doing. Imagine an artist completely lost in a painting. Everything else melts away except the task at hand. This can be achieved through playful games, when learners are completely in the zone (Hari, 2023).

TAKE A MOMENT TO CONSIDER THE LAST TIME YOU USED A PLAYFUL GAME

- What game was it?
- How did it impact engagement?
- What barriers were there?

LET'S UNPICK SOME POSSIBLE BARRIERS ...

WHAT IF THEY ARGUE?

This is often a big barrier. Here's the thing. Sometimes when we play, we disagree. Family Monopoly anyone? This doesn't mean we can't play. We simply need to prepare for these opportunities. We can build these social and emotional skills in micro-teach sessions before the task. We will delve more into that when we unpick regulation. But let's not be scared of arguments. That is like being scared of sadness. They happen. Instead of ignoring, upskill.

WON'T IT BE TOO NOISY?

It won't be silent. But silent classrooms aren't necessarily engaged ones. Of course, we don't want our classroom to be Glastonbury Festival either. This is where routines come in. Explicitly teaching expectations and using strategies such as the voice-o-meter are super-helpful to ensure your classroom is still a learning environment.

DO I HAVE TO DO LOTS OF RESOURCING FOR GAMES?

I used to think I would have to create bespoke laminated games in order to play games. Actually, some games don't require any resourcing! There will be some resources that you always come back to like your whiteboards, sticky notes or dice. Once you start the playful games journey you will also start looking at things in your classroom a lot differently. Magnetic tiles, envelopes and counters will all start to have a newfound purpose. Games shouldn't take you your whole PPA to prepare! I would highly recommend following Liz Ellis from playfullearninggames.co.uk who has a brilliant blog that showcases just this. I would also highly recommend fiveminutemum.com who shows us how little resourcing is needed for playful games too.

HOW DO I EVIDENCE THE LEARNING?

The big question. This really depends on your setting and your senior leaders. We have to ask ourselves why we have to put something in books. Is it for the learners, leaders or parents? The answer depends on possible solutions. If it is for the learners, do they need to see it in their books? Or could you take a picture of them playing and include it in the next lesson? Or could you have a copy of the game on the working wall? If it is for the leaders, is there a better way they can review the planning and learning? Is it for the parents? Do they need to see a worksheet, or could you send them a copy of the game to play? Ultimately, we cannot allow evidence to stop playful games.

IS IT BEST AS A REWARD?

No. It is so easy to resort to 'Okay, well, we will do the worksheet and then a game if we have time.' I get it. But try to reframe. The game is the learning.

WON'T IT GET COMPETITIVE?

The narrative matters. Are we saying, 'Who won first?' Or are we saying, 'Did you have fun?' We can also focus on collaborative games rather than fast-paced competitive ones. Similar to arguments, competitive energy might happen. That's okay, we can support children to build skills. The alternative is never exposing children to games. What often happens there is children find themselves frustrated and dysregulated at playtimes. Social and emotional skill-building should be happening throughout the school day and is essential to learning and engagement.

DOES IT WORK WITH OLDER LEARNERS?

I love games and I like to think I am somewhat of a grown up. Playful games don't and shouldn't have an expiry date.

PLAY + GAMES = + ENGAGEMENT

Children who are excited to learn, will want to keep learning.

HEADLINES TO REMEMBER ON GAMES

- Playful games support children to want to keep learning
- Playful games work against 'the resistance'
- Playful games inject energy and buzz into your classroom

YOUR NOTES ON GAMES

Note down three things you want to remember from this chapter and take forward into your teaching and classroom.

_____

_____

_____

_____

_____

_____

_____

_____

_____

_____

_____

_____

_____

_____

_____

_____

_____

_____

We have a choice. We can cling to a view of human motivation that is grounded more in old habits than in modern science. Or we can listen to the research.

Daniel H. Pink (2011)

I is for intrinsic motivation

CHAPTER 11

'I don't really understand why you're doing what you're doing.'

That was part of my feedback from a lesson observation in my 12th year of teaching. Truthfully? I was exploring. I was exploring how I could tap into intrinsic motivation as a specialist teacher who taught nine classes a week. How could I capture them? What could I create in those 60 minutes that felt so compelling that they would want to be involved? As a specialist teacher I didn't have those well-oiled classroom routines. I didn't know their parents (or the children as well as I'd like!). I didn't even design the classroom I was teaching in. My classroom management relied on a very key ingredient: engagement.

I realised many of my questions led back to myself. But in order to tap into engagement I needed to focus on the children. I wasn't the main character. They were (**and are**). Because, at the end of the day, I can produce a high-quality Broadway show up there. But if they aren't intrinsically motivated to do the task, it's just a waste of a wig!

Oh, and the answer to that feedback was: 'I am exploring the concept of continuous provision with our older learners to experience the theory of flow. I am using strategies to tap into their intrinsic motivation, so they really enjoy learning as opposed to being schooled.'

It was met with some well-masked eye rolls. Which was fair enough. I was going against the grain. But it wasn't something I pulled from thin air. I was just tapping into intrinsic motivation. I had been for the last two years. I had never given out a detention in line with the school's policy. Not every lesson is perfect, we all know that. But for the most part, children were engaged in my lessons. I know that because they were **doing** the task. I know that because it was rather tricky to get them to stop! It was down to our friend: intrinsic motivation.

She's a mysterious concept, isn't she? Even though every school has heard of the term, it is far easier to opt for her sister: extrinsic motivation. Let's demystify the big 'I' shall we?

TRUE OR FALSE?

The reason why you became a teacher was the money.

I'm placing all my bets on false. Because when it comes down to it, extrinsic motivators aren't our core drive. Yes, as we get older, obviously, they do matter. I realise the 'add to cart is a real need! But it's not our core drive, is it? So, what is your core drive for teaching? I wonder, if you've been teaching for a while, has it changed at all?

Why did you want to teach? Why do you keep teaching?

Actually, thinking about our personal drive is something we have to consciously *do* and unpick. As grown ups we might often be having conversations with our friends or our partners unpicking what we really want and why. We can also appreciate that many of us may have experienced a sense of automacy in our lives where it has been less about what we want to do and more about a sense of duty or societal expectation (too deep?). But, for many of us, intrinsic motivation has sat on the reserves bench.

This sense of automacy can be seen throughout our schools. We have to teach the same content in the same way, every day. It may feel like there isn't room for intrinsic motivation on this conveyor belt. However, if we don't make space for intrinsic motivation we are reducing our engagement. Read that again. We then end up trying a bunch of strategies and wonder **why children won't do the work**.

WAIT, BACK UP A SECOND. WHAT ABOUT ACCOUNTABILITY?

As Ana Lorena Fábrega (2023, p. 14) puts it:

> We have resorted to a lot of nonsense in the name of 'accountability'.

We have abandoned intrinsic motivation in schools because the focus became the outcome. Unfortunately, we are all too familiar with needing 'bums on seats'. If this is a new phrase to you, in summary, it is the idea that more children increases a school's funding. In pursuit of this, schools do everything they can to prove to parents that theirs is the best and, often, the proof is in the test scores. As Fábrega (2023, p. 15) puts it: 'Standardised tests are no longer just assessments; they are the point of the whole education system.'

> Bit gross hey?

Let's journey back a bit further to figure out how the heck we got here. Frederick Winslow Taylor. Ring a bell? Well, in the 1900s he developed a factory style to work that was reliant on incentives and threats. Do it right, get an incentive. Get it wrong, receive threats. It was an approach to improve overall effectiveness. And it worked … for a while. Until the twentieth century progressed and the job became more complex, then it was no longer suitable. If the task isn't algorithmic, the process to motivate wasn't simple any more (Pink, 2011).

The issue is, outside this time capsule, many schools (and businesses) are still stuck in this system. Which in turn leaves us stuck in a cycle of trying to *get children to do the work.* But the truth is, if we want children to progress more, we need children to **want** to learn.

THREE DRIVES TO INTRINSIC MOTIVATION

Pink (2011) highlights three drives to intrinsic motivation: autonomy, mastery and purpose. Not to be dramatic, but this research not only changed how I teach but also changed the way I live my life.

AUTONOMY

Autonomy is a cornerstone of intrinsic motivation. It refers to the belief that we have control over our own actions and decisions. In our current school climate, autonomy is a bit of a wild notion, isn't it? It probably conjures up images of children standing on desks with ties around their heads. Here's the caveat. Autonomy doesn't have to mean **full** control.

Let's say your senior leader tells you that you can choose what text you do for your next English topic. You might feel excited, you might spend time really thinking about what will work best. You will be looking at different books and sparking ideas: 'Ooh they could write their own ingredients for a recipe, hey what if they rapped it!' Suddenly you don't notice that you've stayed another 30 minutes or have been working on the weekend. And when a lesson doesn't quite go to plan, you are quick to push through and problem-solve with your chosen text.

If your senior leader hands you a book you don't know and says you must use that for the next six weeks and you need to have a recount, story and non-chronological text … how enthused are you to look through? How much time do you want to spend planning it? And when it goes wrong, how quickly do you want to let your senior leader know that the book wasn't appropriate?

Autonomy shifts engagement because:

- when you choose something, you're more willing to persist with it;
- when you're in control you are more invested;
- when you have control you don't feel as stressed!
- when you choose something, you feel more creative.

MASTERY

Mastery refers to the desire to learn and improve skills. When we feel like we are making progress and becoming better at something, we are more likely to be intrinsically motivated.

A classic example of this is the gym. People become 'gym bunnies' when they start seeing results right? The more we go, the better the results and the more motivated we feel. But let's say (like me) you don't go that often. Maybe you're not really sure what to do when you go to the gym and the classes are always such awkward times. It doesn't feel like you're developing and getting better and that impacts how much you want to go. When we can't visibly see the growth, it can be hard to pull ourselves out of bed.

Mastery shifts engagement because:

- it boosts our self-esteem;
- we feel more excited about challenges;
- we enjoy the process.

PURPOSE

Purpose is the third key element of intrinsic motivation. It refers to the feeling that our actions have meaning and contribute to something larger than ourselves.

Remember when I asked you about why you went into teaching? I imagine 'purpose' was most likely your drive. That feeling of helping a child thrive as their true self. That sense of duty to raise the next generation to know the power of their voice. The idea that, regardless of a child's circumstances we can create a sense of love and belonging for them. The feeling of being a child's champion against all odds. I recently received an Instagram direct message from a child I used to teach. I taught her when she was five and she was now 14. She messaged and told me she missed me, hoped I was well and thought of me often. Purpose is our bread and butter as educators because what we do day to day ripples far beyond the classroom.

Purpose shifts engagement because:

- we are more inspired when we feel like we have a purpose;
- we are way more resilient when we have meaning in what we are doing;
- we feel good about what we are doing!

When we are able to tap into one or more of these drives we aren't asking about the outcome. It becomes nonsensical to the task. I once asked my class: how do you feel that I have never given you a reward? One child said:

'Well, we kind of do have a reward. We have happiness.' Cue tears.

THINK ABOUT SOMETHING YOU LOVE TO DO

- How do you have autonomy in this activity?
- How do you have mastery in this activity?
- How do you have purpose in this activity?

While you're buffering the three drives, you might have some questions pop up.

HOW CAN WE GET CHILDREN TO CHOOSE EVERYTHING?

We can't! In the scrapbook section we will look at the power of 'micro choices'. We cannot get children to choose the curriculum, which class they are in and whether they want to do that subject today. To be honest, too much autonomy can be stressful. Imagine if your senior leader said you could decide EVERYTHING. You would kind of want some parameters, right? But we can give children some autonomy in every lesson, every day which supports intrinsic motivation.

WHAT IF THERE ISN'T A PURPOSE?

Yeah, not ideal, is it? There are some lessons where you yourself are questioning the meaning of life. I get it. But there is (nearly) always a way we can create a purposeful link for our children. Whether it is the way we deliver it or how it correlates to their life or the rest of the curriculum. Again, not everything is going to be a path to enlightenment, but where we can create a bigger picture, our children will buy into it.

WHAT IF CHILDREN CAN'T SEE THEMSELVES GETTING BETTER?

I believe we can make progress and mastery visible all the time. In our mind we might think children will have to go from c-a-t to reading Charles Dickens to feel mastery. The key is not setting unrealistic goals to show mastery. The key is finding the growth in the tasks we are doing and highlighting that. Miles came home recently and said, 'Mummy, I am learning to read.' Because his teacher has explicitly highlighted to them that when they blend, they are reading. Since then, he has started blending words all the time. He's motivated because he can see growth.

MY SCHOOL JUST CARES ABOUT RESULTS; HOW CAN I EXPLAIN THE IMPORTANCE OF INTRINSIC MOTIVATION?

The more we are motivated, the better our learning will be. Intrinsic motivation doesn't have to be an entire new curriculum. It can be tweaks to every lesson that increase engagement. Given the choice, do we want to have children desperate to continue or unwilling to start?

DO WE HAVE TO MEET ALL THREE DRIVES IN EVERY LESSON?

I love the 1 per cent rule. James Clear (2018) often refers to it. It suggests that making small, consistent improvements of 1 per cent each day can lead to significant results over time.

I think this is essential when it comes to teaching. Pick one aspect of intrinsic motivation. Trial it, rework it, try it another lesson and when you're ready … pick another. Think of it as the three drives for you too! Feel the mastery as you see children more engaged, have that spring in your step as you choose what you're going to trial first. Revel in the purpose as lesson after lesson you see an increase in motivation!

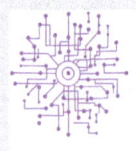 ## THE DRIVE FORMULA FOR YOU …

Purpose = + Engagement

Mastery = + Engagement

Autonomy = + Engagement

Children who have a sense of control, purpose and can visibly see their progress are far more engaged.

HEADLINES TO REMEMBER FOR DRIVE

- Children are more engaged when they are intrinsically motivated
- Intrinsic motivation is more sustainable and effective than extrinsic motivation
- When we have control, we are more motivated to do a task
- When we see our growth, we want to keep going
- When we feel a sense of purpose, we don't want to give up

YOUR NOTES ON DRIVE

Note down three things you want to remember from this chapter and take forward into your teaching and classroom.

_____

_____

_____

_____

_____

_____

_____

_____

_____

_____

_____

A mere hint of belonging is not enough; one or two signals are not enough. We are built to require lots of signaling, over and over. This is why a sense of belonging is easy to destroy and hard to build.

Daniel Coyle (2019)

CHAPTER 12

C is for connect

'This is the best lesson we have had.'

I was struggling. Actually, I need some Caps Lock for this one. I was STRUGGLING. My class were at each other's throats. They would come back from playtime fighting. They would tease each other, intimidate each other and continually put one another down. Really and truly, they felt completely disconnected and lost. They didn't feel a sense of community or connection to each other. Without this, it felt like they **had to** get the upper hand. I could barely start a lesson, let alone get through it without an argument breaking out. My lessons were the opposite of engaging. I kept them working by themselves as much as I could, reduced movement and kept tasks super-closed (like worksheets). I did all of this to try and reduce conflict. But that is where I was getting it all wrong. The first lesson they absolutely loved wasn't on my medium-term plan. I had ordered some furniture for the classroom, and it was delivered to my classroom. As a flatpack. *Insert eyeroll*. Now, I am not the best at DIY, and this felt like the world's worst after-school activity. As I started to examine the boxes in dismay, my class piqued an interest. Before I knew it, children were reading the instructions, getting the appropriate parts, supporting children to balance parts, praising each other, organising themselves like a little team of ants and problem-solving this project. I know it seems like a Disney special, but they made the furniture. Now, I'm not going to lie to you and say we lived happily ever after. It wasn't a magic switch. But it was the beginning of the shift. The shift from you vs me, to us. The shift from competition to team. The biggest shift of all was me. I realised harnessing connection and community is one of the most worthwhile approaches to engagement.

If we know safety and routines are fundamental foundations for engagement, connection is that continual reinforcement of safety. Every time we feel connected, we are reminded we are safe.

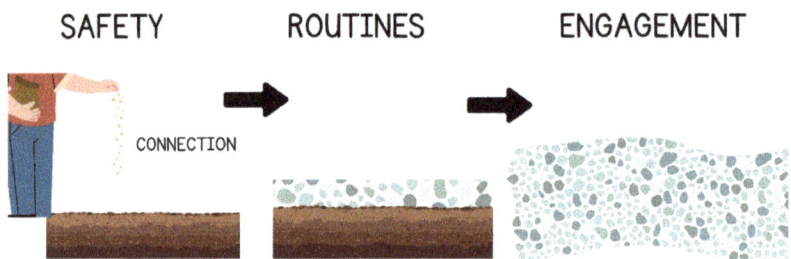

Figure 12.1   Safety, routines, engagement

CONNECTION

Coyle (2019) says that connection cues deliver a steady pulse of signals, telling us we are safe. As we learnt from Chapter 3 on safety, this is undoubtedly fundamental. But let's think about it from our perspective before thinking about our class. I want you to think about past jobs you have had. Jobs you have left. I want you to think about why and whether there is a trend with connection and sense of community. I'll go first! Now, I'm just going to stick to a few teaching jobs, or I would need to create an appendix for exit meetings!

My first school I was at for the longest period of time, five years. You might find it surprising that it was an extremely toxic leadership with a reputation for bullying staff. Why did I stay? I met at least five of my best friends there. I loved seeing them every day, we still talk about hopefully working together again. I laughed every day. I felt connected every day. Ding ding ding. Connection.

Okay, there are three jobs I left for the exact same reason. <u>I didn't feel valued</u>. I had so much to give. I fought for leadership. I shared ideas, I said yes to opportunities, I worked my hardest but … I felt overlooked and undervalued. I desperately wanted to feel connected. But I couldn't reach it.

TAKE A MOMENT TO CONSIDER IF CONNECTION HAS BEEN PLAYING A BIG PART FOR YOU TOO?

- Jobs you loved:
- Jobs you left:
- Any links to connection?

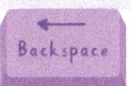

WAIT, BACK UP A SECOND. THE CONCEPT FOR ENGAGEMENT NEEDS A SYSTEM UPDATE

I'm going to use a bit of Monsters Inc.® to explain this if you wouldn't mind indulging me. In Monsters Inc. they believed they needed to collect children's screams for energy, right? They later discovered laughing was an alternative for this. Rather than matching the energy, it actually generated more.

The traditionalist perspective of Western schools is that correction and conformity will establish excellence. (Dating back to those Prussian schools moulding soldiers.) But research shows us that connection is a far more powerful and sustainable way to achieve excellence.

This isn't just in schools. Businesses have traditionally focused on compliance-driven and extrinsic reward-driven systems. Coyle (2019) highlights a company called WIPRO, a call centre in India. On paper, the company was functioning at a high level. It was organised, efficient, provided food and transport for employees and seemed to be working well.

However, they couldn't retain employees and were losing 50–70 per cent each year. They tried the classics: incentives, boosted salaries and awards. Didn't work.

So, they tried an experiment. They explored three different onboarding systems. One focused solely on making employees feel connected. Asking about them, more of a personalised conversation and a personalised uniform. To their shock. This group was 250 per cent more likely to still be working at the company seven months later than the group with zero connection efforts.

Now, obviously, you're not reading this book for retention tips. Let's be honest, we don't hold many cards when it comes to kids attending school. But what is key here is that the employees went from 'being noncommittal to engaged on a far deeper level'. So perhaps we can learn from Monsters Inc here and focus on getting bigger and better results with connection, not correction.

AMYGDALA AND CONNECTION

Science has recently discovered that the amygdala isn't just about responding to danger – it also plays a vital role in building social connections. (Really complements our Monster's Inc. analogy hey?) When we receive a belonging cue – i.e. a smile, wink, touch of the shoulder, recognition, meaningful check-in etc. – it switches the role for the amygdala. It now begins to use neural horsepower to build and sustain social bonds. Basically, when we sense a connection, **we are neurally driven to that**. We do this all the time. Think about your first day of a new job, attending a wedding where you don't know anyone or a training day you had to attend alone. You likely felt a layer of nervousness wrapped around you. But once we've had a little banter with someone, we feel at ease. We then instinctively make an effort to develop that rapport (Coyle, 2019).

WE CAN SHAPE EACH OTHER'S ECOSYSTEMS

I recently had two estate agents come round to my flat. We exchanged little conversation, but when they left, I felt irritated and, actually, a bit upset. This sounds like the world's biggest drama show. But, actually, embodied cognition states how we can impact one another's ecosystems in concrete and physical ways. We may experience a rush of cortisol that elicit our stress response, or spikes of oxytocin that reduce stress. This can happen so quickly! Let me break down this encounter. He was viewing our flat to sell it. As he parked up I shared that we have another parking space and joked about how lucky we were with that space because of my parking skills! He either didn't hear or care! He responded with an eye roll and a 'fair enough'. And that was it. A reach for connection, dismantled, which then impacted the 'weather' of the rest of our interaction and proceeded to impact my mood after. This isn't about adults or children being 'sensitive'. This is an instinctual, primitive, automatic habit. We are continually seeking connections (Hrach, 2021).

FEWER PREDICTIONS, MORE COGNITIVE CAPACITY

Our brain is constantly predicting and surveying for threats. When we are around people, we are unfamiliar with, this dominates cognitive capacity. When we trust and feel connected with the people around us, there is less demand for energy to predict. Remember at university when you were put in random groups to do an assignment? The first few meetings you were probably more focused on how people weren't doing enough, weren't a team player, didn't like you etc. more than the actual topic at hand (Hrach, 2021)!

IMPROVED WELLBEING

I mean, it is kind of common sense, but the research backs it up. We feel happier when we have purposeful social interactions. We can learn from Covid-19 with this. The British Red Cross reported (2020): 'Before the Covid-19 crisis one in five people reported being often or always lonely. Now, 41 per cent of UK adults report feeling lonelier since lockdown.'

A sense of belonging in the classroom is essential for overall happiness in the classroom!

DEVELOPED RESILIENCE

A hill doesn't seem as steep when we are climbing with others.

Hrach (2021)

We are much more likely to approach a challenging task and stick with it if we have a team alongside us. I remember my first Ofsted. I know, it doesn't sound like a great story, does it? At the time, I worked in a federation of five schools. All of the schools rallied together. Educators came from different settings and went through our lessons with us, helped organise resources, and listened! It was such a team. Pizza was ordered, everyone was laughing and cheering everyone on. Even Ofsted can seem jolly with a team by your side!

WE WORK BETTER

Simply put. Research shows, we do our job better when we work in a team we trust (Barrett, 2021).

THE BEST THING FOR YOUR NERVOUS SYSTEM IS ANOTHER HUMAN

And the worst thing. Lisa Feldman Barrett (2021) says 'Our nervous system is bound up with the behaviour of other humans. For better or worse.'

From a classroom perspective, a class is a social environment. We have a group of children in our care. We know categorically children will impact each other's mood. Or connected. We have the choice to lean into connection and boost their engagement and wellbeing at school.

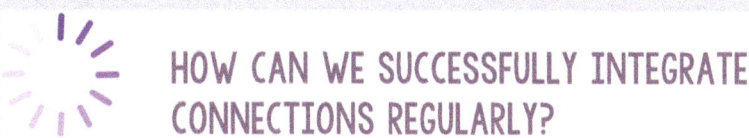

HOW CAN WE SUCCESSFULLY INTEGRATE CONNECTIONS REGULARLY?

RIGHT? I am breaking up our magical manual into three areas: connection cues, partner work and group work. I think these can be done every lesson. Even if you're not doing group work, you can include purposeful partner work and connection cues. I think this is the most actionable way to look at connection and engagement within your lessons.

ISN'T GROUP WORK REALLY DIFFICULT TO MANAGE?

I hear that. As you know from Chapter 4 on routines, I was hesitant to move away from rows and independent learning. I am going to unpick how you can make group work **work**. A system I have used for ages five to 11.

(Continued)

WHAT IF CHILDREN DON'T WORK TOGETHER WELL?

If children aren't working together well, we need to support them to succeed. It is likely because they don't have the social skills. It may be that they haven't done a lot of group work and their brain is predicting danger. Task don't ask is great for this. I know that seems like I am switching gears a bit. But when we use *a task not an ask* in our classroom, our children feel like they are working together regularly. Which means, it doesn't feel like a huge transition to work in a group. BUT there are key scaffolds we can put in place to support you and your children. Coming up in the magical manual!

WHAT IF ONE CHILD DOES ALL OF THE WORK?

A fear I used to have too. This is an indication that perhaps the group task set isn't achievable for all pupils. We can also look at pupil roles, team captains and organisation to get ahead of this.

IF WE CAN IMPACT A CHILD'S NERVOUS SYSTEM SO EASILY, HOW ARE WE SUPPOSED TO MANAGE THAT?

It can feel scary, can't it? You have 30 kids in your class. The last thing you need is to feel stressed about stressing out a child! But here's the good news. Connection cues work both ways. If we can see a child seems out of kilter, we can use connection cues to support them to feel safe, get back on track and engage with the lesson. Don't worry about second guessing yourself, just know you have connection cues in your pocket. Well, in this book at least! Why not, photocopy for your desk and exhale my friend.

CONNECTION/DISCONNECTION

Connected pupils = Engagement

Disconnected pupils = Disengagement

HEADLINES TO REMEMBER ON CONNECTION

- Our children will be physically impacted by others in the class, we can choose how
- We can't force engagement, but we can cultivate connection
- Connection is essential for engagement

YOUR NOTES ON CONNECTION

Note down three things you want to remember from this chapter and take forward into your teaching and classroom.

We feel, therefore we learn.

Mary Helen Immordino-Yang and Antonio Damasio (2007)

A is for attunement

'Ok, I understand what you're saying. But if we carve out all of this time for regulation, how are we going to have time to do the lesson?'

'Well, if they aren't regulated, they aren't doing the lesson, regardless.'

This was a question that came from a TGMC training day with a participant and our trainer Sophie. We were talking about the importance of regulation within the classroom. When we refer to regulation we are talking about a child's sense of balance and control, emotionally and physiologically. Our typical response is that educators feel like it is something 'extra' to do. Which we totally get. It does feel like extra because it's not in the timetable. It feels like extra because many schools and leaders don't prioritise it. But the thing is, there is no lesson without regulation. There is no learning. There is only a giant elephant in the room. As I am planning and writing this chapter it does feel a bit like walking on a tightrope. I have read countless books on engagement, learning and regulation. But very few of them actually bring it all together. If we want our children to be genuinely engaged in the lesson, we **have** to be talking about regulation as part of that formula. We are missing the point if we treat them as isolated concepts. This chapter is about honouring your gut instinct as an educator. So let's get into attunement.

WAIT, WHAT?

Oh yes, you're probably thinking. Attunement? Jen, you've just banged on about regulation for the last paragraph where did attunement come from?

Attunement is like being on the same wavelength. It's about understanding another's feelings and emotions and responding in a way that makes them feel heard and understood. It's giving *Strictly Come Dancing* synchrony. Now, the way that we've been trained and the culture in many schools is that, regardless of what dance your kids are doing, you stick to the plan. Now it doesn't matter if your lesson has intrinsic motivation, playful games and movement ... if children are dancing a different dance, we are wasting our time and energy.

Attunement is like our engagement landing page **and** search engine. Stay with me. It allows us to identify the mood and needs of our class (or a pupil) and match it with an activity that makes sense.

Let me explain attunement in action. I had planned a new project for my Year 4 class. They were going to be creating *You Choose* storybooks for Reception. This was the first lesson to introduce it. I had planned to talk them through the purpose, ignite their imagination through page snippets and share information about how they would approach the project. I was (as I often am, let's be honest) **excited**. It was a bit more teacher-led than my average lesson, but I knew they would love it. It was my first lesson of the day, and we had an impromptu assembly with a speaker coming in (don't you just love that!). Well, this assembly was almost three times the length of our standard time. I sat there looking at the clock thinking there is **no way** I can do this lesson. They can't sit for almost 45 minutes and then come and sit and be quiet again. Even though I knew they would love this project, it just didn't match what they needed right now. So instead, I did this ...

When we got into the classroom, I let them sit where and how they liked. They could chat with their friends or doodle for just under ten minutes. Why? Because they had come straight into school and just sat for 45 minutes. They needed some decompression and freedom. We then played barrier with pages from *You Choose*. I was still introducing the project in some shape or form, but this was a way they could be actively moving and talking. This is attunement. This is not something I would EVER have done in my first or second (or third) year of teaching. Because the mindset was: stick to the plan. But what would happen if I kept calm and carried on? I would be faced with a slow and rocky lesson that left me headfirst in my snack drawer. We need to teach, encourage and support educators to attune to their pupils. Because that is how we get the best out of everyone!

How are we feeling right now?

Results show the best activity is...

Figure 13.1   How are we feeling right now?

ATTUNING TO NEEDS

We do this all the time. We wake up and, where we can, we make decisions based on our needs. We cancel dinners when we need quiet. We go for a walk if we need energy. We run a bath if we need to relax. We put our phone in the next room if we need to focus. We order some food if we are tired. As adults, we are attuned to ourselves. And, where we can, we make small shifts and choices.

Where we can't, we reserve the right to be irritated if we don't have that choice. Ever begrudgingly gone to a staff meeting you know isn't relevant to you? It can be very tricky as adults to have a game face on. BUT we work through this because we can rationalise it and reframe the situation:

> We are paid to do this job and that includes all meetings even if they don't serve me.
> I will plan tomorrow's lesson within the meeting … sneakily.

TAKE A MOMENT TO CONSIDER WHEN WAS THE LAST TIME YOU REFRAMED?

When was the last time you attuned to your needs/how you were feeling?

How did you feel?

What did you decide to do?

When was the last time you had to do something that wasn't attuned to your needs?
How did you rationalise and reframe to continue?

Our children don't have this luxury. That part of the brain that helps us to rationalise is our prefrontal cortex. This part of the brain isn't fully developed until we are 25 years old. So, if our children aren't feeling it, their feelings override anything else.

We can understand this too from our own experiences. Sure, there are times we can switch on our game faces. But we've all had moments where our dysregulation has trumped the rationale. I remember firing up my computer ready for teaching and seeing an email pop up. It was from my senior leader. It read:

> *'Can you pop in and see me after you've finished teaching this morning. Thanks.'*

Did your heart start beating fast too? No? Just me then. I had three hours before I finished teaching. Three hours of spiralling thoughts. I wonder if you can predict how my lessons were that morning. I was on edge. I wasn't myself which impacted my patience and my delivery. I had raincloud energy which created a stormy climate in the classroom. I had to keep teaching, and I couldn't rewire. By the way, the meeting was actually about me doing **too much work**. Which, indeed, was a first for me and was absolutely not included in my spiralling thoughts! Think about a time you weren't able to attune to your needs and your dysregulation trumped rationality.

TAKE A MOMENT TO THINK ABOUT WHEN DYSREGULATION DERAILS THE SITUATION

- Can you think of a time you were dysregulated (or off balance) at school? Why?
- How did it impact your teaching?

This happens for our children **all** the time. They have to be at school, on the carpet, sitting quietly, doing the work and there are rarely (if ever) opportunities to support their needs, to ensure they are actually engaging in the lesson. This then escalates into undesirable behaviours and a lack of learning. Attunement is about understanding our children are human and if we want the best engagement out of them, we need to focus on their needs before our lesson plan.

WAIT, BACK UP A SECOND. HOW DOES EMOTION FIT INTO LEARNING?

The role of emotions in learning is fairly a new concept. The first educational book I ever read was *Emotions, Learning and the Brain* (Immordino-Yang, 2015). It was at this time, ten years ago, I was leading regulation as a whole-school initiative. I vividly remember leading a staff meeting sharing how brain scans illustrate the impact of mindfulness in reducing our stress response. I (perhaps foolishly) invited everyone to do a body scan. Let's just say the eye rolls were pretty intense. This is something that has been a bit of a journey. The research is there. However, the research in neuroscience, psychology and mental health is filtering down very slowly into the education sector. Immordinio-Yang says herself (2015) that she wanted to **start the conversation** as to how we can use this research to look critically at the curriculum we present to our pupils. Today, the role of emotions and learning is commonly understood, which weirdly we have Covid to thank for (sorry for saying Covid). But how we apply it effectively in school becomes a bit pixelated.

'The relationship between learning, emotion and body state runs much deeper than many educators realize and is interwoven with the notion of learning itself.'

Immordinio-Yang (2015)

When we talk about engagement in school, the conversation often circles around children who are focused and on task and children who are not. When we talk about emotions in school the conversation often circles around children who manage their emotions or don't. What if we brought both conversations together? We are going to look a bit further at a range of regulatory experiences children may have and how understanding that can help us meet their needs and enhance engagement.

IGNORING THE FEELINGS OR ENERGY DOESN'T HELP

As Kate Silverton says, it isn't about stopping the energy. It is about meeting a need (Bryce-Clegg and Silverton, 2023). We've be trained to plough through the lesson and follow it to a T. Needs don't disappear. Big feelings get bigger if you ignore them (Ruby's worry taught us that!). We can't just 'will' children to change their energy. We have to meet it. That is what attunement is all about.

Figure 13.2   Michael Rosen on emotions (Rosen, 2016)

AROUSAL STATES

Kim Griffin (2023) shares helpful insight into 'arousal states' in her book *Success with Sensory Supports*. I have adapted her arousal bar below. Arousal refers to the level of energy in the body. This directly influences our ability to pay attention.

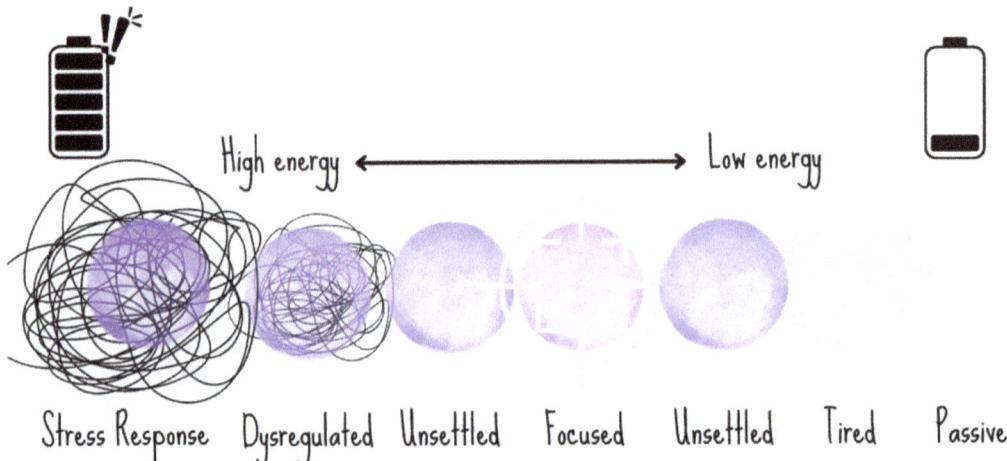

Figure 13.3   Stress bar

Griffin (2023) explains that to be able to learn, the brain and body need to have the right level of arousal for the task. If the arousal is too high, our prefrontal cortex cannot process effectively. Ever had a child bust into the classroom saying they have a playdate that day and continue to mention it throughout the day? It's a lot of energy and excitement in the body! Equally, I once was teaching and there was a monitor lizard (I'm not joking) outside our classroom. Well, I can tell you we didn't finish reading *The Monkey Puzzle*. What about when it starts snowing? The list goes on. We have all experienced high arousal in the classroom and know full well the impact it has on engagement (to the task that it is!).

In contrast, if arousal is low the brain will not have sufficient focus and attention to learn. It reminds me of when my partner teacher and I would try to solve a cover issue at the end of a day's teaching. Nope. Can't compute. We've all been guilty (don't leave me hanging) of talking for way too long and looking out onto a sea of blank faces.

Griffin (2023) emphasises that all arousal states are okay! This isn't about being calm all the time. We need to acknowledge the energy in the room and respond accordingly, which is what attunement is all about.

WHICH SYSTEMS ARE ACTIVE IN YOUR BODY?

Sensory Solutions (Thoonsen and Lamp, 2021) further illustrates what our body needs through its *sensory fan model*. This focuses on particular sensations in the body. A child (or class) that is under-responsive will benefit from more activating strategies, whereas a child (or class) that is over-responsive will benefit from more calming strategies. In general terms, children function most effectively in the active system. Thoonsen and Lamp (2021) echo Griffin (2023), stating that being on different sides of the fan does not necessarily mean it is a negative thing – it's based on context. For example, a child might feel a surge of stress heading into a swimming competition, but this adrenaline and tunnel vision will likely aid their performance!

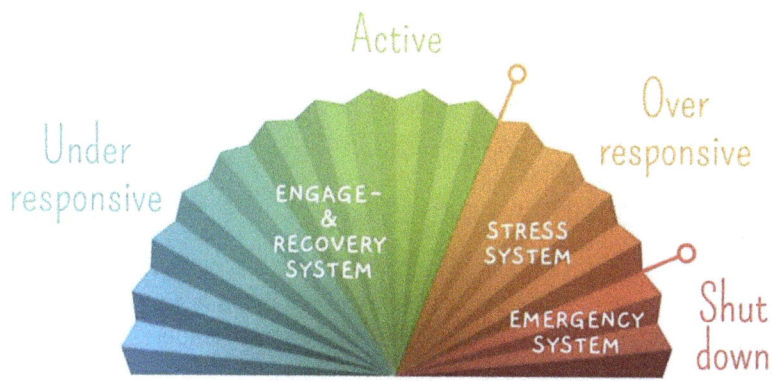

Figure 13.4   The sensory fan model (Thoonsen and Lamp, 2021)

We can attune to our children's arousal and system levels in the classrooms to support engagement. For example, if we know our class is feeling under-responsive (low arousal levels) we can choose a high-energy activity like a game, movement or collaborative task. If our class is presenting as over-responsive (high arousal levels) we can choose an activity that will calm their bodies such as a story, whiteboard task or sensory rest. Being attuned to our children's sensory communication can optimise engagement. For example, I used to use *zones of regulation* (Kuypers, 2011) routinely for registration. For those who aren't familiar, this is a regulation framework linked to colours (see below). Children would communicate which colour they felt like. This gave me a great opportunity to attune! If the majority of my class said yellow, I might choose to get the wiggles out before starting the activity. Or I may choose to do a calming transition buffer to calm their bodies. Totally dependent on how they were responding and attuning to what they needed there and then. I will share more 'tuning in' activities in the magical manual.

Figure 13.5   Zones of regulation (Kuypers, 2024)

 ## THINKING THROUGH QUESTIONS ON ATTUNEMENT IN THE CLASSROOM

WHAT DOES THIS LOOK LIKE IN THE CLASSROOM?

Attuned engagement is about reading the needs of your class and adapting your activities to suit their level of energy and current emotional states. It is also about setting up for success and embedding empathetic classroom routines that support safety and emotions.

DO I HAVE TO CHANGE MY WHOLE LESSON?

No. We aren't wizards. It might be as simple as having an attunement buffer like silent reading to calm or a movement break to wake up. It might be a change in the main activity like the project lesson I talked about at the start. In our magical manual section I will show you how we can attune for engagement. Sometimes I like to think of attuning as quite literally 'tuning an instrument'. Just taking a moment to ensure your class is actually ready for the lesson. In the magical manual we will look at buffers and adapters. Buffers are a short task you can do before you continue to attune to the needs of your pupils. Adapters are ideas to adapt the task to suit the needs of your pupils.

WHAT IF IT IS ONLY ONE CHILD?

You might find that a child has come into the classroom and is in need of activating or calming strategies. In this situation we can still attune to their needs. However, it doesn't *need* to be a whole-class shift. They can use activating or calming buffers in a calm space/ reading corner/outside with a teaching assistant.

WHAT IF IT IS A HANDFUL OF CHILDREN?

I once had a group of girls who were in a *Gossip Girl* feud. They were completely focused on who could give the best 'evil eyes' across the classroom. They would whisper about each other, side-eye until the cows came home and basically do anything they could to make it ***known*** they weren't friends. I didn't have a teaching assistant, but I knew there was no point in them being on the carpet as they weren't learning. I gave the class a whiteboard task and asked the girls to come to the book corner. I said it seems like there is a whole lot going on and I want to support them. I then sent them to separate tables with regulation tools and a journal template to share their side of the story. While they were doing that, I could finish teaching, set the class on the task and then support the peer conflict. It sounds much easier said than done, of course, but we *can* stop and support children. It doesn't have to be on the spot, but what is important to note is you can adjust your lesson to reflect the needs of your children at any point.

(REGULATION + NEEDS) X ENGAGEMENT = LEARNING

HEADLINES TO REMEMBER ON ATTUNEMENT

- Children can't engage in the learning if they aren't regulated
- Attuning to our children's needs is investing in the learning
- Slight tweaks to your lesson based on your class energy can improve engagement

YOUR NOTES ON ATTUNEMENT

*Whether people achieve expertise is not some fixed
prior ability, but purposeful engagement.*

Robert Stenberg (quoted in Dweck, 2007)

L is for the ladder

CHAPTER 14

'We don't have place for you in the sixth form.'

When the teacher input is over, what is it that keeps children focused, engaged and thriving? I started secondary school in the lowest of four sets. It wasn't until my GCSEs that I realised an E grade wasn't for excellent and G wasn't for good. It probably surprised my teachers that I did get into sixth form. I did get into university, and I did graduate with a first honours. Let me be clear. This isn't just a nice paragraph for me to have a humble brag. This illustrates EXACTLY what we should be instilling in our children. It wasn't because I was born with a certain set of skills or intelligence. It is because I truly believed I could do these things if I kept trying and explored different angles. Many of my teachers told me I couldn't. I wasn't 'sixth form material'. But this was their narrative, not mine. This is the element we seem to be missing from the classroom. It is about instilling a growth mindset and a toolkit for resilience if we want children to engage with the learning long after we have finished talking. We want children to be resilient. But how can we really achieve this as part of our school culture and daily habits? How can we ensure it is a beating heart of the curriculum rather than a wistful aspiration?

WHAT DO I MEAN BY THE LADDER?

This chapter is about giving children the skills to continue to engage with the learning when you are not sitting right next to them. To pull themselves up. To build a skillset that supports them to thrive. It is about shaping their mindsets for what learning should really feel like and encouraging them to take the next step with grit. If you have ever felt like you are working harder than your children, this chapter is for you. It is about supporting your children to stay engaged during independent learning without leaning on you to energise that.

WHY WON'T THEY JUST DO THE WORK?

Ever done a brilliant (if we say so ourselves) teacher input, but then experienced one or two children that simply don't start the work? I mean, the audacity of it. Am I right? The thing is, if children think they can't, more often than not, they won't. And I think if we are all being honest with each other, that isn't just about children. Like, humour me. Have you ever had a big project/deadline or task that you know you will find difficult and just kept reshuffling it to the bottom of your to-do list? Same my friend.

For our children, this feels far more overwhelming. Picture having to do that task, and 29 other people are doing that same task at the same time as you. You all have different starting points with what you know and the skills to hand. Oh, and they will be judged afterwards, potentially publicly. Time ... starts ... now. Anyone want to dash for the door?

On top of that, our children simply have fewer experiences to fall back on. That unknown element (remember our safety chapter) creeps in and the unknown feels far too scary to take on. As they see other children start the task their confidence continues to plummet and their vulnerability increases. The feeling of potential inadequacy overrides everything else and the lid simply stays on the pen.

My point is, when a child doesn't start the work, there is so much more going on. A child's mindset towards a task is one of the biggest barriers to 'giving it a go' and it is about time educators were armed with PRACTICAL tools to support that.

As Dr Carol Dweck (2007) brilliantly describes, most of us have experienced a childhood where we viewed IQ as the whole story. There was a shared understanding that we are dealt a certain hand when it comes to intelligence and that is fixed. Now this is a heavy and mighty task for educators. Because, as Dweck highlights in her Ted Talk (2014), brain scans show that when children with a fixed mindset meet an error or hurdle there is little brain activation. They don't try. They run from it. This may relate to your experiences at school. I know it did for me for most of my schooling. Until I realised it was the obstacle between me and becoming a teacher. Not getting into sixth form would mean not teaching. I had to teach. I believed it was what I was meant to do. And that was where my growth mindset stepped up. However, you may have been 'in a top set' at school. That might have impacted your mindset and your relationship with school.

TAKE A MOMENT TO THINK ABOUT YOUR EXPERIENCES
AND THE IMPACT THAT HAD

- What was your understanding of intelligence at school?
- Were you considered 'intelligent' as a child?
- How did that impact your attitude to learning?
- What type of mindset did you have?

GROWTH MINDSET

Dweck's concept of *growth mindset* (2007) tells us that the ability to learn isn't fixed. It can grow through effort and that failure is not a permanent position. We now understand the impact of having a growth mindset. We know that this increases brain activation. We know that when we view challenges as an opportunity for learning and push through, we build strong neural connections. Dweck shares incredible insight into 'typical' underperforming students that failed year on year in Harlem, New York (2014). She shares how adopting a **growth mindset classroom** led them to score in the 95th percentile in the National Test where many of them couldn't hold a pencil at the start of the year. This is just one example of many studies that showed growth mindset surpassing pupil starting points. Integrating a growth mindset attitude in our classrooms changes how our children view effort. Instead of shutting down, they **engage**.

SITTING IN THE STRUGGLE (DR BECKY)

'You're fine.' 'Come on get started.' 'You know what to do.'

As educators (or parents) if our children say they can't do it our instinct is often to tell them they can. This is us genuinely wanting the best for our kids. It is instinctual and it shows how much we care. Dr Becky Kennedy (2022) shares that this shows how much we want our children to succeed, but actually resilience comes from our ability to tolerate tough feelings, not get out of them. This means sitting in that struggle with our children. Stepping into that feeling with children and showing that we aren't scared of the feeling and problem-solving with them removes those possible feelings of vulnerability and even shame. This shapes the struggle as a challenge, not a shortcut to failure. Remember what we learnt in Chapter 12 on connection? A climb doesn't feel so steep when you are doing it together.

DON'T BE A SHINING KNIGHT

When you cut it for me, write it for me, find it for me, open it for me, tie it for me, all I learn is you do it better than me.

Unknown

When we see a child struggle, it is instinctual to rescue them. (I mean, depending how 'teacher tired' we are of course.) Let's not disregard the added pressure of time constraints in a school. Getting to assembly on time, finishing the work before play etc. If we see a child struggling it isn't weird to want to jump in and fix it for them. You are certainly not alone in that feeling if it resonates. Dr Lucy Foulkes (in Bethune, 2023) highlights how anxiety surrounding a challenge is maintained if we don't experience the journey through it. If our children are anxious about writing a sentence and we write it for them, that anxiety hasn't gone anywhere and will likely pop up again the next time they need to write a sentence. However, if they have a toolkit to work through that struggle – i.e. word mats, sentence starters, talking tins etc. – that is how they can move through it and experience success. This supports their schema of challenges. As we noted earlier, children have fewer experiences than us. The unknown creates more anxiety. We can build experiences of resilience, and this supports them to know they **can** do it and increases engagement.

THE STRETCH ZONE

Figure 14.1   The stretch zone

Developed by Tal Ben-Shahar and shared by Adrian Bethune in *Wellbeing in the Primary Classroom* (2023), the stretch zone is the concept that getting children to step out of their comfort zone is the best way to achieve their fullest potential. When children operate in the comfort zone, the work is not challenging for them. In many cases this may cause boredom and disengagement. Adrian explains how the stretch zone is where children's neurons will be firing and wiring, where they are flooded with happy hormones which support high engagement within the task. You have probably guessed it, but the panic zone is very much a stress response which we learnt all about in Chapter 3 on safety. Providing the right level of challenge is how we can support engagement.

GRIT

Angela Duckworth highlighted in her famous Ted Talk (2013) the very key message of this book:

> *I came to the conclusion that what we need in education is a much better understanding of students and learning from a motivational perspective, from a psychological perspective.*

Duckworth carried out multiple studies to explore what was the driving factor for success. Her results showed that it wasn't IQ, talent, looks or social intelligence. It was grit. Duckworth describes grit as looking at learning as a marathon, not a sprint. As educators, it can feel like a bit of an eye roll. I mean, a fast-paced curriculum, six lessons a day, two-week writing cycles, need I say more? The education system is built for the hare not the tortoise. But Duckworth shares this is the key to success and stamina. Think back to that child coming straight up to you as soon as it is independent learning time. Grit keeps them engaged in the task. Duckworth shares her support of *growth mindset* as a core strategy to building grit over time.

NEUROPLASTICITY

Back in the day, we would assume that after a certain age our brain has done all the firing and wiring and, basically, retires. Well, neuroscientists are now certain that our brains are elastic. Regardless of our age, brains can continue to be shaped and developed. We all have the power to develop our neural connections and learn new things. Why does this matter for engagement? Knowing this and having our children know this, supports the understanding that you're not wrong. You're just en route to the right answer. This keeps the wheels turning rather than pulling into the garage.

HOW ON EARTH CAN WE SUPPORT THIS IN THE RUSH OF THE SCHOOL DAY?

You're not wrong. We do need leaders on board. We need our school leaders to understand investment in a growth mindset culture and a resilience toolkit is an investment in our children long term. Horrible answer, right? Aside from putting this book on their desk, in our magical manual I will share some daily practical tools you can use to develop this culture.

WHAT IF THEIR PARENTS OR GUARDIANS HAVE A COMPLETELY DIFFERENT MINDSET?

We are all doing the best we can with the tools available to us. Let's get elastic ourselves and think about how we can take our parents on this journey with us. Maybe it is parent workshops or newsletters. Maybe it is bringing them into the classroom. It could be sharing some of your growth mindset tools with them. Ultimately, control the controllables.

WHAT IF RESILIENCE CAUSES LOTS OF BIG FEELINGS AND MELTDOWNS?

Honestly, it naturally does. And if you are thinking this you are already winning. Why? Because for children it isn't the big feeling that is the worst. It is being alone in that feeling. It is the shock of that feeling. If we know it might trigger some tricky feelings, we can prepare for that as a class. We will unpick this more in the magical manual!

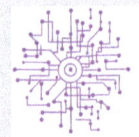

GROWTH MINDSET, RESILIENCE, GRIT, ENGAGEMENT ...

When we foster a growth mindset the engagement continues

HEADLINES TO REMEMBER ON LADDERS

- Cultivating a growth mindset keeps children engaged through challenges
- If we want to develop independence, we need to establish resilience toolkits
- Engagement has to come from the child, not from us

YOUR NOTES ON LADDERS

Note down three things you want to remember from this chapter and take forward into your teaching and classroom.

Part 2

Engagement needs a boost? Ask these 10 questions and then flip through your Magical Manual for activities to hand.

1   Do children feel safe?
2   Are routines clear?
3   Can all children access?
4   Do I need more movement?
5   Have I included tasks within input?
6   Am I incorporating games?
7   Are children intrinsically motivated?
8   Are there enough opportunities for connection?
9   How can I attune to my class here?
10 Do children have the tools to stay engaged?

CHAPTER 15
SAFETY BEFORE MAGIC
CLASSROOM ESSENTIALS

SETTING UP FOR SAFETY

Safety is the pedestal for engagement

Visual timetable

Greetings

What?

A visual timetable is literally what it says on the tin. It is a visual way of displaying the day, so children know what is coming up next.

Why?

Take away the unknown. If we don't know what is happening, that makes us feel unsettled. Set the scene for the day to support children to feel a sense of safety.

What?

A chance to informally check-in with your children and a connection-based routine. This is just standing at the door and taking a moment to greet each child.

Why?

Checking in with children will provide an opportunity to support them if they're feeling a bit wobbly. The routine connection will support trust and safety.

Morning routine

Non-verbals

What?

A predictable first 15 minutes of the day does wonders for supporting children to feel safe. It might be a greeting, check-in, soft start and registration. Try making the morning predictable.

What?

Non-verbal signals are a classroom staple to allow children to communicate to you at any time.

Why?

Predictable routines require less troubleshooting which creates more capacity for engaging learning.

Why?

If children feel like they can't communicate their needs this will (understandably) feel stressful. Non-verbals take that out of the picture.

READY, SET, REGULATION

Ten regulation ideas for children who need to feel a sense of security

Doodle

Two to four minutes of free doodling can support a child to decompress and be ready to engage.

Read

Three to five minutes of reading quietly can support a child to regain their balance. Especially if they have a favourite book!

Head on the desk

Simply allowing children to rest their head on their desk or pop on some noise-cancelling headphones can generate a sense of calm and safety.

Fidget

If a child needs to feel a sense of security, it might be because their mind feels quite busy. Fidgets can help support children to be in the present moment, clearing their mind.

Sensory tool

Similar to a fidget, a sensory tool is something specifically sensory-related like playdough, Lego, or kinetic sand. These engage the senses which can help the mind feel focused.

Wall push

Encourage a child to push against a wall. This redirects energy in the body positively, allowing them to engage in the lesson.

Grounding exercise

Give yourself a hug, rub your temples, or stretch up high. Utilise your body to feel different pressure points and relieve tension.

Colouring

Some children will benefit from two to four minutes of free colouring. This creative expression can support regulation on the spot.

Breathing mat

Utilising the breath is the most impactful thing we can do to regulate. Breathing mats are really helpful to make this child friendly and enjoyable.

Change of setting

Sounds simple, but can shift a child's mood, comfortability and sensory input.

CHAPTER 16
THE PATH TO MAGICAL ENGAGEMENT

CLASSROOM ESSENTIALS

MAAT ROUTINES

Movement around the classroom

When you are doing engaging activities, it may involve getting out of your seat or walking around the classroom. Clear routines for this help these activities to be efficient and successful.

1,2,3

Originally a Ruth Miskin strategy, this is used for successful transitions. When you show one finger children stand up, two fingers they turn to where they're going, three fingers they walk and sit down. This can be varied and used for a range of transitions in and out of the classroom.

Gradual start

One of my favourite routines. If you are about to start a big engaging activity, do it one group at a time and share specific (positive) feedback on how they followed the instructions, i.e. went to the right area, sat down straight away etc. This supports your class to see a live example rather than just auditory instructions.

Job roles

If part of the activity involves getting equipment, it is helpful to have clear job roles for this. You don't want 30 children huddled around the glue sticks. This doesn't have to be elaborate; you could have team captain badges, printouts, or tokens. Give them to one person in each group/on each table to be the collector!

Path plan

Sounds ridiculous but if you have a small classroom you might decide to have a walking path plan. Hear me out. It works for escalators in London, and it can work for your classroom. This is a directional path or walking plan for your class. For example, always clockwise. This ensures all children have personal space and can get from A to B easily. This isn't necessary for all classrooms but if you find your children bump into each other a lot, or your classroom is smaller than average, this can help!

MAAT ROUTINES FOR ENGAGEMENT

Assigning tasks

If we're doing engaging tasks, it is likely that there will be some collaboration and group work going on! One routine that can be helpful is assigning tasks. Take out the guesswork for some of these systems. As children are exposed to more collaborative work these social skills will improve, and you will find routines are less needed.

Table plans

Number, letter, or symbolise children's seats – i.e. A and B, 1 and 2, circles and triangles. Or you could get creative, linked to your school, like bees and sunshine. Regardless of what you choose, have it on your tables permanently. This might be a table sticker or tacky-backed icon. This way you can say: 'If you are a bee, you are writing first' or 'Sunshines, you play the part of Macbeth'. Easy assigning for partner work!

Equipment placement

Simply place the equipment in front of a specific child. For example, if the scissors are in front of you, you will be in charge of cutting.

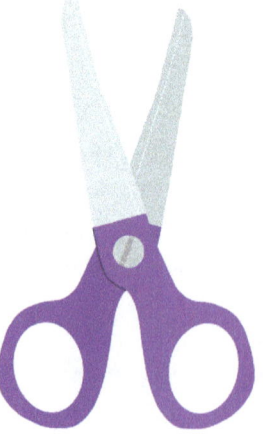

Class captain

Again, really helpful. Having class captains during engaging tasks allows you to have a group of mini teaching assistants. You can give them a clear focus and because it's always random, every child gets to be that leader.

Quiz it

Give your children a quiz. Like decide who is one or two. Or one of you put your hands on your head and one of you on your shoulders. Because this feels algorithmic it doesn't require much discussion, and children feel like they can make the decision quickly without deliberation. You can then say, 'Okay number ones, you are cutting'. Basically, associate the quiz with the roles! You can do this with groups of three, but it becomes more of a fuss with bigger groups.

MAAT ROUTINES FOR ENGAGEMENT

Attention getter

We can't do engaging tasks without an attention getter. If we set them off and can't bring them back together, we get ourselves in a bit of a pickle. There are so many attention getters, but here are six you can come back to. It can be helpful to remind and practise before you set off on the task!

Instrument

Tambourine, bells, whatever you have hanging around. Hear it, and freeze!

Stopwatch

Create a routine where you put a timer on the screen for an agreed time. Mine was always 1 minute 20 seconds! When children see it, they come to the carpet. I would always put it on and then walk around the room prompting with a hand on shoulders. Let social contagion do its thing!

Visual cue it

Holding your hand up, wiggling your fingers, putting a photo of the children sitting on the carpet on the board are all great silent attention getters!

Call and response

Are you ready? YES, WE ARE.
Hocus pocus! EVERYBODY FOCUS.
Hands in the air ... like you just don't care.
The list goes on! There are endless possibilities. I used
to create one linked to activity, for Where is Alice?
WONDERLAND.

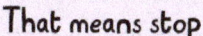

That means stop

Clap it

Do I need to say more? Make up a clap and get children to
copy. Take it down to two fingers and then mime the clap.
This will get the attention and then keep it!

Body percussion

Shoulder tap, clap, click and repeat.
Children will love to join in, and you can try and challenge
them by changing it up. A great one for getting and keeping
attention!

MAAT ROUTINES FOR ENGAGEMENT

Transition instructions

When children are in the midst of an engaging task and we need to share some instructions or more information, we need to have a routine to make that seamless rather than continually telling children they need to listen!

Hands on your head

Really simple, but if you need to give children instructions that will take less than a minute, just ask them to put their hands on their heads while you're giving it. Model this too! That way, you know when it feels too long!

Freeze and flexible

FREEZE is to get everyone's attention and flexible is so children can sit in a comfortable way if you need to talk to them for more than a couple of minutes. You can have an action for this so children know.

Instruction point

Bring everyone back down to the carpet for tables. This environmental cue will change the pace and allow from better focus.

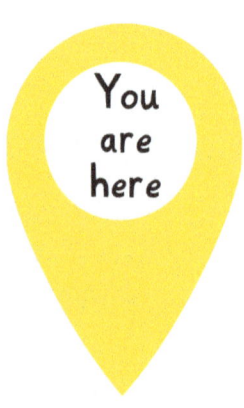

You are here

Listening maps

If you need to call the children for a longer period of time (think about their developmental attention span) use listening maps. This is when children have a whiteboard and write down what they understand from the instructions. This keeps hands busy, minds focused and a paper trail of the instructions!

Type it

Simply type instructions on the board during the task. Use an attention getter, and ask children to read silently or to read in their groups. No more than five points on a slide for cognitive load!

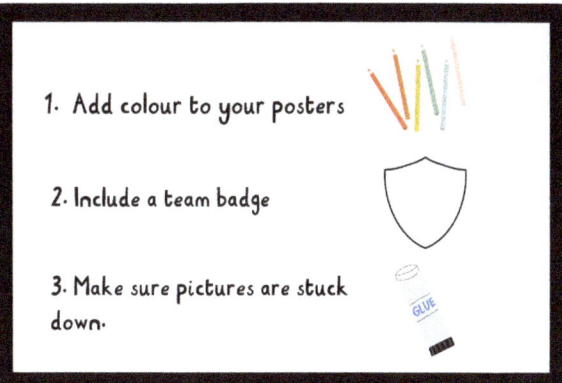

1. Add colour to your posters

2. Include a team badge

3. Make sure pictures are stuck down.

RE-ESTABLISHING ROUTINES GAME

Routines are for life

Have these games in your toolkit so you can easily re-establish routines before a task, in less than five minutes.

Freeze frame

Getting children to freeze frame what a good or bad routine looks like is super-effective because:

- children are processing visually what the routine looks like
- children get to visually process other children's live examples
- unpicking whether it is a good or bad example supports greater depth of thinking.

Picture perfect

One of my favourite reasons for using planning systems like Canva and Google Slides is that you can instantaneously upload photos to your slides. This means you can use examples of children doing it perfectly and unpick it as a class. This works because:

- children get to see themselves as the experts
- it taps into prior experience
- it is visual.

Word dump

Give children a routine or expectation and have them generate as many words as possible linked to it. This works because it:

- focuses on collaboration
- builds on learning
- taps into prior knowledge
- generates the success criteria.

group work, calm, share, take turns, listen, respect

RE-ESTABLISHING ROUTINES GAMES

Routines are for life

Think it, draw it

Give children a routine or expectation and have them draw what a good one looks like! This works because:

- it allows children to process independently
- it is visual
- it provides a variety of visual examples
- it supports dialogue.

Mind the gap

Give children a routine or expectation and have the success criteria underneath. Remove certain words and have children discuss what the gaps are. This works because:

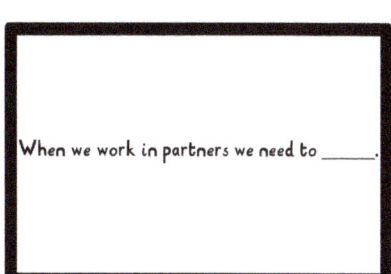

When we work in partners we need to _____.

- it supports vocabulary
- it allows pupils to collaboratively generate success criteria
- it develops processing of the routine.

Thumbs up, thumbs down

Before an activity or routine, list behaviours and ask children whether they should or should not be doing the behaviour. Ask them to show their thumbs. This works because:

- it collectively outlines the expectations of a task
- it is time-effective
- it gives children the opportunity to process the boundaries before beginning.

CHAPTER 17
BODY CHECK
Classroom essentials

BODY CHECK

Six gestures to enhance engagement

When saying a number, show it on your hands to support memory and increase attention.

Use open arms when delivering new learning. This supports excitement.

Put a finger to your head when showing you need to remember something. This associates that learning with the action.

Put your hand under your chin and look up when thinking. This encourages children to also stop and take a pause.

Use a thumbs up and/or smile when teaching as this signals recognition and community.

Signal your hands back and forth to show that you and the class are a team when talking about a challenge.

Nine ways to incorporate pattern difference

Remember, pattern difference is all about pick'n'mix to evoke engagement.

Hunch your body towards children to gain attention.

Point to something like a display.

Pick up something concrete related to the learning.

Kneel, move to a seat or sit down on the carpet for part of your teach.

Circulate, move as you teach. This creates more interest and focus.

Freeze! When saying something super-important to double down on that messaging.

THIS IS... IMPORTANT.. BECAUSE...

Change your delivery by slowing your pace to emphasise certain points.

Change your delivery by speeding up your pace to convey excitement.

Exaggerate a facial expression to connect emotion to the meaning.

BODY CHECK

Three rules to remember

As we know, children need to know they are safe before they engage. Your hands are a key signal for this. Simply showing your hands supports a sense of safety.

When working with children, sit next to them side by side rather than front on as this is less threatening. Once again, safety is the road to engagement.

Research actually shows that 60/70 per cent eye contact feels safe. We also need to think about the differing needs and preferences of our neurodivergent children. So don't force eye contact and don't expect children to constantly track you either. It actually detracts from engaging.

CHAPTER 18
THE STORE CUPBOARD
Classroom essentials

YOUR ENGAGEMENT STORE CUPBOARD

Fold this page!

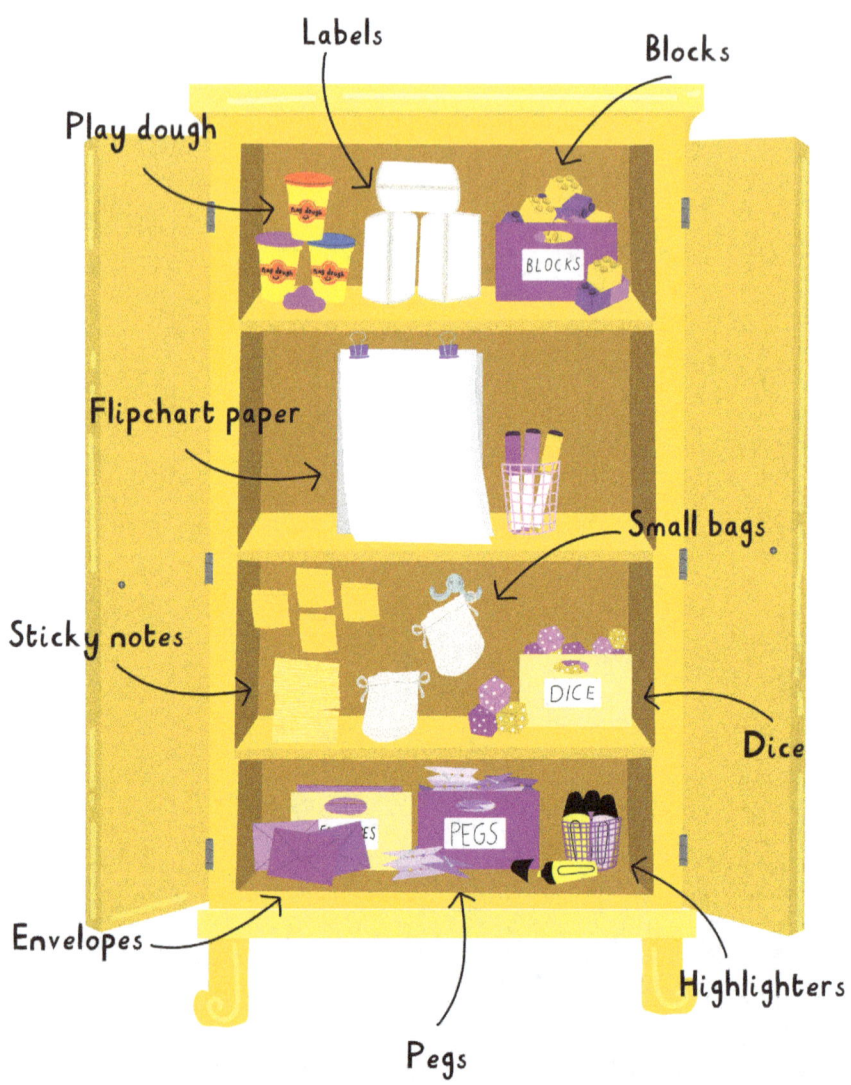

Labels

Blocks

Play dough

BLOCKS

Flipchart paper

Small bags

Sticky notes

DICE

Dice

PEGS

Envelopes

Highlighters

Pegs

Item: play-dough

Five ways to use it:

recreate what you remember

maths representation

tactile storyboarding

letter formation or spelling

visual representation (anatomy of a plant).

Item: labels

Five ways to use it:

storyboarding

non-chronological reports or posters

organising maths questions

editing work

match up definitions to pictures

bonus: stick onto blocks for more uses, like number sentences.

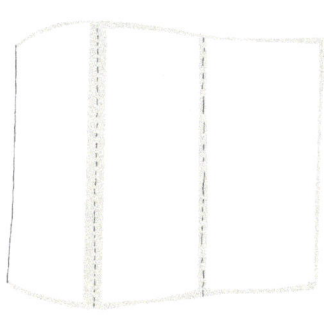

THE ENGAGEMENT STORE CUPBOARD

Item: envelopes

Five ways to use it:

group tasks/challenges

mystery puzzle or text extract

match up tasks (i.e. answers and number sentences)

sorting and organising (word classes, numbers etc.)

secret images for playing barrier.

Item: pegs

Five ways to use it:

building words on string (letters on pegs)

number sentences on string (numbers on pegs)

peg and string timeline

peg sounds to matching images

label pegs for organising images or text extracts
(i.e. true or false, primary or secondary).

Item: highlighters

Five ways to use it:

editing work

word hunting (i.e. adverbs)

annotating pictures

organising posters or reports

peer assessment - play the teacher.

Item: flipchart

Five ways to use it:

mind mapping

role on the wall

collaborative non-chronological reports

organising or sequencing

collaborative presentations.

THE ENGAGEMENT STORE CUPBOARD

Item: blocks

Five ways to use it:

- build structures or recreate scenes
- use as maths manipulatives
- create a tactile timeline
- physical oral blending
- sentence building.

Item: sticky notes

Five ways to use it:

- sequence events
- generate ideas and then group or rank them
- oral blending
- bookmarking learning (i.e. prepositions in books)
- annotate pictures or sources.

Item: small bags

Five ways to use it:

guess what is in the bag, with clues

themed learning kits

mystery questions

props to inspire storytelling or sequence a story

inside is the answer, what was the question?

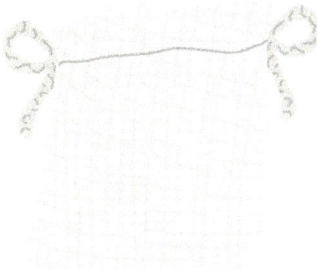

Item: dice

Five ways to use it:

roll and solve: have a grid linked to maths questions

roll and write: have a grid linked to vocabulary

roll and tell a story: have a grid linked to pictures

roll and investigate: have a grid linked to artefacts

roll and investigate: have a grid linked to changing variables.

CHAPTER 19
NEUROAFFIRMING
CLASSROOM ESSENTIALS

NEUROAFFIRMING ESSENTIALS

Fold this page!

Modelled example

A modelled example can take a verbal instruction and make it concrete. When we can see what success looks like, it reduces anxiety and increases engagement.

'I need' bookmark

An 'I need bookmark' allows children to communicate their needs so they are able to engage in the task. It is a checklist with common needs listed, for example quiet, movement, blanket, etc.

Now, next, after

An essential resource for chunking tasks and supporting cognitive load.

Communication signals

Embedded communication signals in your classroom reduces anxiety and supports classroom flow as children can communicate at all times.

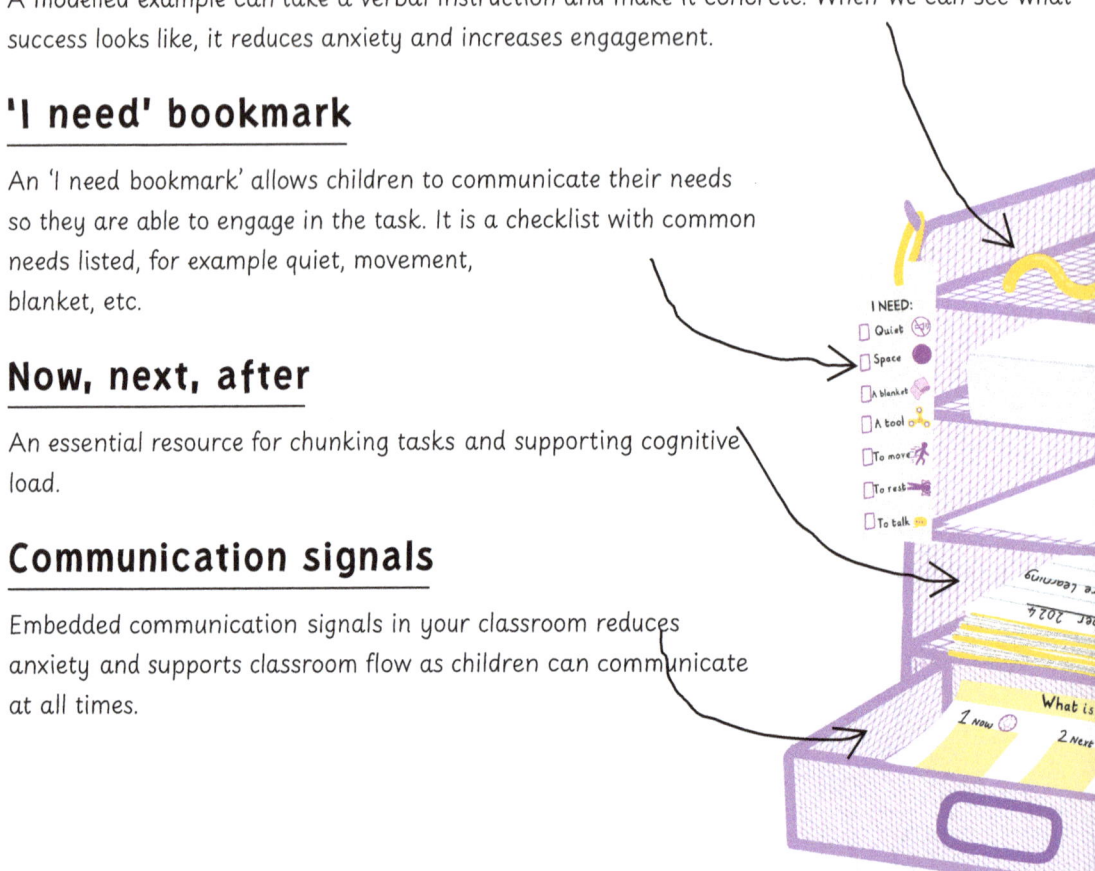

Timers

Provide structure and predictability which can help reduce anxiety and improve focus. Can support in a chunking of tasks.

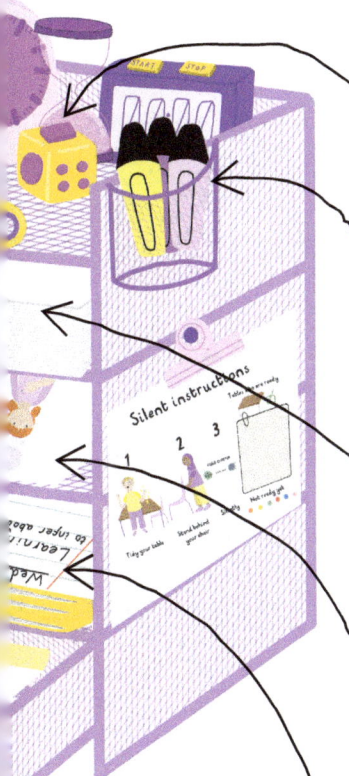

Fidgets

Fidgeting supports energy exertion, providing sensory stimulation and redirecting focus.

Highlighters

Improve focus and visual organisation. Children might need to highlight key words or parts of a question.

Whiteboards

Support children to practise, doodle and add a tactile element to learning.

Visuals

On slides and on resources, visuals support all children to process faster and more effectively.

You will need

Before children start the task, it is helpful to have visuals of what they might need – scissors, coloured pencils, etc. This supports organisation, focus and seamlessly starting the task.

CHAPTER 20
M IS FOR MOVEMENT
CLASSROOM ESSENTIALS

FLEXIBLE SITTING

Let's start as we mean to go on

Age range: all ages

What is it?

If we know movement is important to learning, we need to first break the mould of stillness. The concept of flexible sitting isn't a new one, but it hasn't dropped firmly into all education systems. Yet. It is the concept that there is not one uniform way of sitting to be upheld all day long.

When can I use it?

Any time children are having to sit. Let's lean into body autonomy, flexibility and comfortability!

Why does it work?

When our children are comfortable, they are more likely to be focused and sustain engagement. Flexibility also supports autonomy which is a key indicator for motivation.

Steps

1 Explain to children that sitting comfortably in class is essential for focus, happiness and learning.
2 Show children the posters and ask children to sit in each sitting position; for younger children you can use the chant from your posters.
3 Talk about comfortability and ask children to rate (perhaps with thumbs up/down) how they feel in each position.
4 Share safety boundaries, i.e. keep hands close so not to get stepped on!

Simplify

You may choose to have fewer options. Choose which seating positions are applicable for your classroom.

Challenge

Ask children if there are any other positions they feel comfortable in and discuss whether they are safe and appropriate for the classroom/all lessons.

TEACH ME, TELL ME

Get children to do the work

Age range: six+

What is it?

Teach me, tell me cards are a way for children to teach each other subject-heavy info! Here's how it works. Each card looks similar to the one below. The idea is that children go around and ask another child their question. They can either tell them or ask to be taught! If they knew the first answer, ask the challenge question. It is key to only have around six questions circulating so children meet the same questions and become experts!

Created by Excitingteacher in collaboration for Brain School.

When can I use it?

This is a perfect strategy when you have a lesson that is very 'content-heavy' and you don't want to do death by slides! This works for ANY subject!

Why does it work?

It gets children moving, collaborating and thinking! It is also brilliant for self-esteem as children feel a sense of achievement. The gamification element keeps children at all levels engaged!

Steps

1   Create your cards linked to your learning. You can use my template.
2   Quiz children on all the questions on the cards. Thumbs up, thumbs down style (i.e. thumbs up if you know the capital of India).
3   Play teach me, tell me! You can use these slides to introduce. Children can play independently or in pairs.
4   Finish with the quiz again. Watch children feel super-proud and confident this time!

Simplify

- Use fewer questions
- Have children work in pairs
- Add visuals to your card

Challenge

- Use more questions
- Have children work individually (although pairs support a collaborative approach)
- Give children a recall time to write or draw everything they remembered on the tables!
- Use trickier vocabulary and give children a word mat

WALK AND TALK

Remix a classic

Age range: all ages

What is it?

I don't think anyone can head into teaching without being fully aware of what 'partner talk' is. This is a movement-based remix where we get all the goodness of partner talk PLUS all of the movement and collaboration benefits.

When can I use it?

You can use this in exactly the same way you would use partner talk. Which injects movement and energy immediately into your lesson with very little effort or prep!

Why does it work?

This does wonders for engagement because it automatically increases blood flow to the brain. If the question is right it taps into dopamine, oxytocin and endorphins! One of my favourite things about this is it is really structured so it makes management easy peasy!

Steps

1   First you want to make sure you have a good open-ended 'discussion-based' question.
2   Get children to stand up.
3   Use a signal (I use a reception bell) like an instrument, clap or sound.
4   When you use the signal, children walk around the room silently.
5   When you use the signal again, children talk to the people nearest them (either twos or threes).
6   Rinse and repeat until you tell them to walk back to their seats.

Simplify

Give children a sentence starter for each time they meet a partner. This will help with their oracy and your formative assessment! For example: 'I think the character is feeling xx.'

Challenge

Have question choices on the board so they can choose which question and to keep it interesting.

RELAY RACE

It's giving team spirit

Age range: all ages

What is it?

This is my ultimate replacement for a worksheet. It turns a solo task into a movement and collaborative one. Take your worksheet and blow it up to A3 and photocopy for each group (ideally four). Stick the worksheet around the room and ask children to stand in a line facing that worksheet. The pen is the baton! They take turns completing something from the worksheet, pass the baton and go to the back. When they have completed they all sit down.

WORKSHEET

When can I use it?

Best for closed task worksheets. For example, match it activities, grammar focused, mental maths, ordering events etc. Once you start you will realise the mountain of opportunities. You can use it for your starter, your exit task, to break up the teacher input or even before the main task!

Why does it work?

It works because children are up and moving which increases alertness. It also works because there is a 'safe' gamification element. It feels like a game, but a game where you have a team by your side. Which leads me to the next WHY: it aligns with collaboration and connection which support engagement.

Steps

1   Choose an appropriate worksheet task (let them see it on the board first).
2   Blow up to A3 and stick around the room.
3   Sort children into groups of four to six and have them vertically face the wall.
4   Take turns passing the baton to complete the task.

Simplify

- Give children 'huddle' time to support each other before the task
- Allow children to go up in pairs or have a coach who stands and helps each player

Challenge

- Have different tasks for each group so it focuses on the learning in a different way, i.e. match it, fill in the gap, draw a picture to show the meaning
- Give children a chance to 'magpie', have one magpie visit each group and talk to them and come back
- Have children allocate a 'teacher' to go to another group and mark

JIGSAW GROUP WORK

Make them the experts!

Age range: five+

What is it?

Ever felt like you have so much teacher-led content to get through and you wish you could skip to the interactive stuff? Sometimes we just have subject knowledge-heavy lessons. But that doesn't mean we have to lose all engagement. Jigsaw is a way to make the children the teachers. Give each group a piece of information (a piece of the jigsaw if you will!). They learn it. Nominate one messenger. The messenger goes to each group and has two minutes to tell them their information. The group then has two minutes to tell the visiting messenger. By the end of the jigsaw. Everyone knows it all!

When can I use it?

Any subject-heavy lessons! It lends itself well to topic-based lessons; history and geography work well. Anything where you have too many slides.

Why does it work?

The change of face keeps it interesting. The idea that your group has exclusive information makes it exciting. The fact that you retell your information to different messengers supports that long-term memory and, of course, the collaboration keeps it fun!

Steps

1   Have six questions on the board and ask children to rate their knowledge.
2   Have the answers to those six questions prepared in your chosen form. I tend to put them in envelopes!
3   Tell children that in their groups they have the answer to one of the questions and they need to learn it.
4   Make sure all groups are confident before they nominate their messenger.
5   Model how the messenger will go around the room and use a timer for both the group and the messenger to teach.
6   Bring everyone together and ask them to rate their knowledge on the six questions again!

Simplify

You can use *talking tins* or *buttons* for younger children: one per group, with an exclusive fact. You can also use photos – for example, photos of the most popular food in a country – for them to identify and share with groups.

Challenge

Use text and inference for them to figure it out first rather than just telling them.

THE SCALE

Where do you stand?

Age range: all ages

What is it?

A simple, unthreatening movement activity. Give children an opinion-related question and create a scale in your room. You can use whiteboards or paper to label each side. Or you could just tell them. For example: Goldilocks was bad, true or false?

When can I use it?

For any two-option opinion-based questions within any lessons!

Why does it work?

The movement aspect increases the energy in the room. It is the whole-class activity which has a social contagion aspect to it. It increases participation as you can visually see your peers' opinions rather than asking everyone individually.

Steps

1   Ask a question (or series of questions).
2   Point to the choices.
3   Ask children to silently walk towards their opinion. It doesn't have to be a complete (yes) or a complete (no) it might be somewhere in the middle.
4   Summarise the key findings from the scale!

Simplify

Ask one question at a time and bring back down to summarise to support structure and management.

Challenge

- Ask children to talk to the people next to them on the scale and see if they have the same reasoning
- Partner up children on different sides of the scale to debate
- Add masking tape and give children a sticky note to write their reasoning to put on the scale.

FOUR CORNERS

A touch of cardio

Age range: six+

What is it?

A similar energy to the scale, but four corners is basically about creating an interactive game show. You come up with a list of questions with four multiple-choice answers. Children need to silently go to the corner of the room they think the answer is.

MOVEMENT

When can I use it?

Great for starters and consolidating knowledge in a movement-focused way. It is also a great end to the lesson activity to pull together new information.

Why does it work?

Because children are active, not passive. If they don't know the answer, they soon will and it is a quick and effective way to formatively assess.

Steps

1 Prepare your questions (five will work a treat).
2 I would recommend having the questions on a slide so children can process visually and on an auditory level as you read them out.
3 Give four options (a,b,c,d or 1,2,3,4).
4 Ask children to walk to the area of the room where they think it is the answer.

Simplify

- Scale back to three corners and three multiple-choice answers
- Have children play in pairs

Challenge

- Ask children to justify their answer to the people nearest to them
- For older children, nominate children to come up with a question linked to the lesson and four multiple-choice answers

READ AND MOVE

What it says on the tin

Age range: five+

What is it?

Generally, teachers in 2025 use slides or some sort of reference to teach right? Let's add some movement spice to that. Identify words that children will physically interact with. Simply colour code a selection of words and give children a rule – i.e. when you see a word in 'purple' please stand up.

When can I use it?

Any time you are reading from anything that the children can see!

Why does it work?

As we know, sitting is the new smoking. So, getting up regularly is going to naturally increase that engagement.

Steps

1   Pick which words you want to highlight.
2   Colour code them.
3   Choose your rule.
4   Start reading.

Simplify

- For younger learners you may choose to get children to read key words after you
- Add sound buttons to support early readers

Challenge

- Stand up and read
- Clap and read
- Echo whisper
- Act out the word

BALL TOSS

Everyone loves a prop!

Age range: all ages

What is it?

I mean, you may have guessed it from the title. Toss a ball! Literally, bringing a beach ball into your discussions and using it to ask children's opinions, votes, one-word answers quickly and effectively enhances engagement.

When can I use it?

Anytime you need to wake up your class. If you notice children are looking a lil sleepy, ask a question and grab the ball!

Why does it work?

The physical movement can increase energy levels and mood. The social interactions (and especially chain sentence stems) support belonging and connectedness.

Steps

1   Think of a question.
2   Decide whether to use sentence stems.
3   Make the rules clear – i.e. not passing to the same person, safe underhand throws.
4   Play ball toss!

Simplify

- Start with a roll in circle time
- Just use one-word opinion answers at first for children to feel safe and for everyone to get a turn

Challenge

- Nominate a child to become the key questioner
- Add chain sentence stems – i.e. I think playing outside is better than inside because I can run more. What do you think, Jen? (Throw the ball to Jen.)

GRAFFITI

But, keep it legal

Age range: all ages

What is it?

Prepare yourself. Writing on the table. If you have been doing a task at the carpet or silently, add some creative movement by asking children to write their thoughts, reflections or feedback directly on table with whiteboard pen. Note: this is obviously dependent on what tables you have, please check first!

When can I use it?

After a teacher-led input, independent task or partner task. Basically, when they've got something to say about something!

Why does it work?

It's really about moving into a change of environment which works wonders for reducing fatigue. It is also about tapping into novelty and excitement which is great for engagement!

Steps

1   Think about your focus: reflection, ideas, mind mapping etc.
2   Give children a key task – i.e. 'Write or draw everything you remembered, create a story map, mind map your ideas etc.'
3   Ask children to write on tables!

Simplify

- Draw pictures that come to mind
- Draw what comes to mind while a teacher is reading
- Work in partners or as a group

Challenge

- Give children a chance to view others through an 'exhibition walk' (see next activity)
- Highlight or underline similar words or pictures to their partner/group

EXHIBITION WALK

Shhh!

Age range: all ages

What is it?

If you want children to see each other's work, but you don't want to unleash chaos. The exhibition walk is for you. Basically, you tell children they are now in a museum. We can't talk in a museum. You put some calming music on and children can walk around the tables observing the 'work'. You can even get children to take their shoes off for this to support grounding.

MOVEMENT

When can I use it?

After an independent or group task or project where you want children to share their work in a calm way.

Why does it work?

Moving around increases engagement and alertness. We've all had children present things one at a time with instant regret! The novelty aspect supports excitement and if your shoes are off too that is going to support regulation!

Steps

1 Tell children they are about to do an exhibition walk and recap the rules!
2 Put some calming music on and maybe a picture of a museum on the wall.
3 Encourage children to take their shoes off.
4 Enjoy the walk!

Simplify

- Give children a focus like 'find a great adjectnes'
- You could even ask children to take a whiteboard and whiteboard pen and have a task as they go on the walk

Challenge

- Give children sticky notes to write positive feedback and stick by the work
- Allow children to write compliments directly on the table
- Have half of the group on the exhibition walk and half of the group presenting their work/ interacting with the guests and then swap

SNOWBALL

High energy alert!

Age range: six+

What is it?

Sounds wild, but the children LOVE it. Snowball is when you give children a task that has legs. For example, how many nouns can you think of? Or name things you can do outdoors. Things you might see in Ancient Rome etc. Ask them to write as many as they can in a given timeframe (one min should suffice). Then collectively scrunch up the paper. Launch it. Collect a snowball and add it to it.

When can I use it?

As a starter or a recap at the end of the lesson.

Why does it work?

Throwing, moving, scrunching ... all of these include our body in the learning process. Not to mention it is just super-fun.

Steps

1   Give children a thought prompt.
2   Give children a timeframe to write as many ideas as possible.
3   Scrunch the paper.
4   Throw the paper.
5   Collect a snowball.
6   Open up and add ideas.
7   And repeat!

Simplify

Have children work in pairs.

Challenge

- Have a whiteboard and write down most common words
- Create sentences with the most common words

FLOOR WORK

Take it to the floor!

Age range: all ages

What is it?

No mystery here. It is simply doing the activity on the floor instead of at tables. Even better? Allowing children to lay on their tummies and take their shoes off. Obviously. In the spirit of flexible sitting this is an option not a requirement.

When can I use it?

Whenever children are doing independent, partner or group work.

Why does it work?

Lying down supports relaxation which is great for mood and engagement. It is also a novelty so makes it more desirable. Generally lying on your tummy closes off some peripheral vision which supports focus.

Steps

1   Think about your task and if it is suitable.
2   Check for space and create options, where needed, by moving things around.
3   Offer the opportunity to your children.

Simplify and Challenge

No need to simplify or challenge here – the key component is choice.

PLAY-DOUGH

Everyone loves play-dough. Fact

Age range: all ages

What is it?

There are lots of ways for children to share during lessons, many which we are unpicking together! Drawing, writing, standing, talking ... but what about making? I started doing this in my second year of teaching and have done it with every year group. Simply give children some play-dough and a task to demonstrate their learning. It might be, what do you remember about the story? What was the most important part? What are the parts of a plant?

When can I use it?

Whenever children are reflecting or processing their learning.

Why does it work?

The tactile exploration engages the senses. The experience can also reduce distractions and provide regulatory input.

Steps

1   Think about a key question for exploring.
2   Share your play-dough rules (these will be particular to you and your class).
3   Give the play-dough!
4   Put some music on to double down on the chill.

Simplify

Give each group a specific focus or criteria – e.g. everyone on this table is recreating solid particules.

Challenge

- Work as a partner or group, this is actually more challenging as children need to share their vision and work as a team to recreate
- Extend to stop motion to recreate a concept

NON-VERBAL QUIZ

More fun than it sounds

Age range: all ages

What is it?

Children have been sitting, you have been talking, let's inject some movement in three, two, one:

1   What do you think the correct answer is? Hands on your head if you think xxx. Hands on your shoulders if you think xxx. Stand up if you agree. Wiggle your fingers in the air if you'd feel the same way. You don't have to open the question up, but it immediately involves children.

MOVEMENT

When can I use it?

Any time you're talking and want to add engagement. Add a question and get them to communicate their thoughts without speaking.

Why does it work?

Instant movement, instant engagement. Doing something all together as a class increases a sense of community and fun.

Steps

1   Ask a question.
2   Give a non-verbal way to respond.
3   Summarise what you see.

Simplify

Have agreed non-verbals; you might have an image for this as a classroom display. This helps to remind you and acts as a cue to children.

Challenge

- Expand further: why do you agree? Tell your partner
- Write why on your whiteboard

PAUSE AND PLAY

No screen time involved!

Age range: all ages

What is it?

Who loves a freeze frame? This is a twist on that. Pause and play allows children to pause and show you an expression and feeling and then play it out. What would be the first words that they say?

When can I use it?

When looking at different perspectives. Specifically focusing on role play. This will fit nicely into English lessons, but also any lessons where you are talking about someone else such as PSHE.

Why does it work?

Involves your whole body freezing into a position and then thinking about what that would communicate. It is whole-body learning in all the best ways.

Steps

1   Think about a person or character's perspective.
2   Ask children how that person or character might be feeling.
3   Say you are going to say PAUSE and they need to pause in that expression and feeling.
4   Ask children to think about what they are thinking or what the first thing they might say is.
5   When you say PLAY children can either say it, whisper it, tell a partner or write it.

Simplify

• You may choose to start with the pause and develop that before the play!
• Take a photo and add it to your slides! Annotate together or print out for the next lesson
• Ask children to do it with partners

Challenge

• Get children to play it out in groups for longer periods and letting the situation unravel through live inference
• Watch each group and use a 'remote' to pause and dissect the 'scene'

CHAPTER 21
A IS FOR: A TASK NOT AN ASK

CLASSROOM ESSENTIALS

TASK DON'T ASK: NON-VERBALS

Culture shift

What is it?

This is a culture shift that supports classroom communication. Use Makaton symbols and signals for key phrases to ensure children can talk to you at all times with minimal disruption.

Toilet

Talk to you

Drink

Can you say it again?

Can you help me?

Can I ask a friend?

TASK DON'T ASK: WAIT TIME

Culture shift

Age range: all ages

What is it?

How quickly we can process a question depends on many factors: the complexity of the question; the prior knowledge of the pupils; and the language used in the question. What we do know, however, is that less than three seconds ain't gonna cut it. Wait time is the understanding that we should wait at least ten seconds to support processing. This can be utilised within our tasking. Set the task, ask children to think about it before you expect them to begin. Even better if you can model that thinking process.

TASK DON'T ASK: WHITEBOARDS – WORD COLLECTION

Let's generate ideas

TASK DON'T ASK

What is it?

Ask children to collect as many words as they can linked to a topic. They can do this independently or with a partner.

Subject ideas

Maths: An ask: how do you know it is subtraction?
A task: which words are associated with subtraction? Write as many as you can on your whiteboard.

English: An ask: which word triggers an emotion for you in this text?
A task: write down any words that trigger an emotion.

RE: An ask: what do Jewish people eat during Rosh Hashanah?
A task: write as many things you remember about Rosh Hashanah.

Science: An ask: who can give me an example of a material?
A task: write down as many materials as you can think of.

History: An ask: what can you tell me about a school day for an Ancient Egyptian child?
A task: write as many words as you can linked to the school day for an Ancient Egyptian child.

Geography: An ask: what is climate change?
A task: write as many words as you can linked to climate change.

Mix it up

- Work with a partner
- Circle similar words
- Do it alphabetically
- 'Stand up if you wrote down this word'
- Build it into a sentence
- Illustrate the words
- Turn it into a table
- Rank it from most important to least

TASK DON'T ASK: WHITEBOARDS – DRAW IT

Express yourself

What is it?

Instead of talking about the answer, ask children to draw their understanding.

Subject ideas

Maths: An ask: how do you know it is subtraction?
A task: which words are associated with subtraction? Write as many as you can on your whiteboard.

English: An ask: what did the tiger eat?
A task: draw what you can remember the tiger eating at Sophie's house.

RE: An ask: what symbols are there for Christianity?
A task: draw one or more symbols for Christianity on your whiteboard.

Science: An ask: what are the four seasons?
A task: can you draw four pictures that represent the four seasons on your whiteboard?

History: An ask: can you describe a Viking boat?
A task: draw a Viking boat.

Geography: An ask: what is an example of physical geography?
A task: draw an example of physical geography.

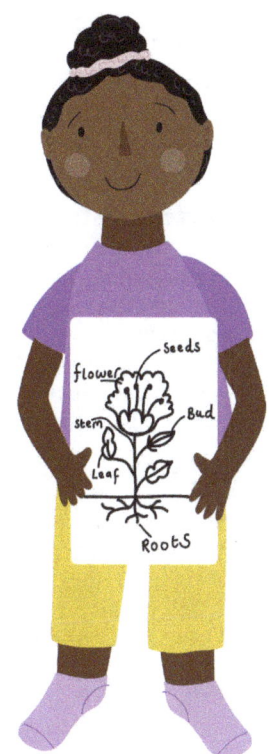

Mix it up

- Work with a partner
- Add annotations
- 'Stand up if you drew xx'
- Walk and talk (but walk and share!)

TASK DON'T ASK: BIGG PARTNER TALK

Like partner talk, but better

What is it?

Ever set children off on a partner talk and it feels like they have nothing to talk about? Or you hone in on one couple of children to work with and before you can say anything most of the class have finished? This is where BIGG partner talk comes in.

B – better questions
Think about questions that children can actually discuss rather than one-word answers.
I – invitation to talk
Give them examples of their sentence starter or possible discussion topics.
G – gamify
Tell them how to get to the next level!
G – group response
Don't then ask children one by one to feedback. Do a global task before moving on.

Subject ideas

Maths: An ask: what is the first step to solve this problem?
A BIGG task: can you sequence the steps to solve this problem with your partner?
You might be saying: 'The first thing I would do is …'
If you have identified the sequence of steps, start solving it with your partner.
I saw and heard it many times. The first thing you did was u, u u, u ? (underline) the key words. Exactly!

English: An ask: look at your school uniform. What sound does jumper start with?
A BIGG task: you and your partner are going to identify the first sounds in what you are wearing.
Let's start with our hands on our shoulders. You might be saying 'Hmm, what does jumper start with.'
Once you've identified the sound, look at what else you are wearing!
I saw lots of you point to your shoes which begin with a, say it with me, shhhhhh.

Science: An ask: what food chain might start with grass?
A BIGG task: you and your partner are going to think about an animal that eats grass.
You might start with, 'One animal I know that eats grass is …'
If you've done that, I wonder if you could think of the next animal in that food chain?
So many great food chains; can you draw them on your whiteboard?

Mix it up

- Draw or write on your whiteboard what you discussed
- Walk and talk with your partner
- Stand up if you said xx
- Join another pair and see what similarities/differences you have

TASK DON'T ASK: CLAP ONCE, CLAP TWICE

Moving and grooving

What is it?

If you have a question with two choices, rather than asking children 'What would you choose?' Ask them to clap once for one option and twice for another.

Subject ideas

Maths: An ask: would you use a number line or column addition?
A task: if you'd use a number line clap once; if you'd use column addition clap twice.

English: An ask: what features help you read this text?
A task: which feature do you think helps you read the text easily? Clap once for bullet points and twice for images.

Science: An ask: what do you think is more important, diet or exercise?
A task: what do you think is more important, diet or exercise? Clap once for diet and twice for exercise.

History: An ask: which Greek temple do you think is better?
A task: would you prefer to visit the Parthenon or Athena's temple? Clap once for Parthenon and twice for Athena's temple.

Geography: An ask: what excites you about Lunar New Year?
A task: what is more exciting for you? Clap once for red envelopes and twice for making lanterns.

Mix it up

- After they clap ask them to put their hands on their head to support management!
- Do it in a circle, spot someone with a different point of view and match up for a discussion
- Split the class into one claps and two claps and do a quick debate!

TASK DON'T ASK: WAVE IF YOU THINK . . .

Keeping it neighbourly

What is it?

Get children's opinions and thoughts quickly by asking them to wave if they agree. Instantly triggers that sense of community and fun too!

Subject ideas

Maths: An ask: which fraction would you prefer to have of this pizza?
A task: I'll read the fractions, you wave to show me which one you want for the pizza!

English: With reference to *The Day the Crayons Quit* (Daywalt, 2014).
An ask: which crayon do you think has the best argument?
A task: I will say the colour of the crayon, wave for the one with the best argument to Duncan.

Science: An ask: which circuit is going to light a bulb?
A task: I will point to each circuit. Wave when I land on the one that lights the bulb.

History: An ask: which ruler do you think was better?
A task: I will say their name; you wave when you hear the name of the best ruler.

Geography: An ask: which of these are countries and which are cities?
A task: I will say the name. You wave when you think it is a country.

Mix it up

- Write down why
- Draw why
- Share with your partner why

TASK DON'T ASK: CLASS WAVE . . .

Actually, something completely different

What is it?

This is a way for everyone to verbally say their answer. Basically, you hold out your arm straight in front of you. You twist your body slowly 180 degrees. When children are directly in line with your arm they share the answer. Similar to a Mexican wave in a stadium!

Subject ideas

English: An ask: can you think of a rhyme for this sentence?
A task: share your rhyme when the wave rolls to you!

Science: An ask: can you think of a carnivore?
A task: share a carnivore when the wave rolls to you!

History: An ask: what do you think helped them win the battle?
A task: share a word or two about why you think they won the battle when the wave rolls to you.

Geography: An ask: which landmark would you be most interested in visiting?
A task: let me know which landmark you'd like to visit when the wave comes to you.

Mix it up

- Stand up when they say it
- Whisper it
- Freeze frame it (if it is to do with an emotion or action)

TASK DON'T ASK: SHOW ME THE NUMBER

Hands at the ready

What is it?

So simple and so easy to execute. Instead of asking children a question, give them a multiple choice. Number the options and ask children to show you the answer with their hands.

Subject ideas

English: An ask: which would be the best way to punctuate this sentence?
A task: number three options – i.e. full stop, exclamation mark and question mark – and ask children to vote.

Science: An ask: which material would you use for a rain jacket?
A task: number three options with pictures – i.e. silk, cotton and polyester – and get children to vote.

History: An ask: which vase tells us about everyday life?
A task: number each vase and ask children to vote.

PSHE: An ask: what do you think Louisa should do next after receiving this message? (Link to cyber bullying.)
A task: share three visual scenarios and ask children to vote.

Mix it up

- After the vote children can all say it at the same time
- See if they match their partner and discuss why or why not
- If there was another option, what could it be? Draw on your whiteboard
- Have children draw, write or discuss what the options could be before sharing and voting

TASK DON'T ASK: WHISPER IT TO ME

Shh! Keep it down

What is it?

Really easy to do on the spot and perfect for those closed questions. Simply ask children to whisper the answer to you.

Subject ideas

Maths: An ask: which number is odd?
             A task: whisper the odd number to me.
English: An ask: which one is the adjective?
             A task: whisper the adjective to me.
Science: An ask: which is the liquid?
             A task: whisper the liquid to me.
History: An ask: which item would you see in the Victorian period?
             A task: whisper the item you'd expect to see in the Victorian period.
PE: An ask: which muscle groups are we working?
             A task: whisper which muscle groups we are working.

Mix it up

- Whisper to your partner
- Mouth it but don't say it

TASK DON'T ASK: TELL ME IN THREE, TWO, ONE

We're all in this together

What is it?

Another great option if you want children's involvement with a closed question. Simply say 'you tell me in three, two, one'. This is best to use when you know children are super-confident with the answer.

Subject ideas

Maths: An ask: which shape is regular here?
A task: have a think whether this is regular or irregular. Tell me in three, two, one …

English: An ask: is it a statement or a question?
A task: have a think, is this a statement or a question? Tell me in three, two, one …

Science: An ask: is this a vertebrate or invertebrate?
A task: have a think about whether this is a vertebrate or invertebrate. Tell me in three, two, one …

History: An ask: is this a primary or secondary source?
A task: have a think whether this is a primary or secondary source. Tell me in three, two, one …

Mix it up

- Tell your partner in …
- Tell the floor in …
- Say it to the window in …
- Tell your hand in …

TASK DON'T ASK: THUMBS UP, THUMBS DOWN

Do you agree?

What is it?

A great task for when you want children to vote their opinion quickly and in a hassle-free manner.

Subject ideas

Maths: An ask: is this a prime number?
A task: I am going to say some numbers; thumbs up if it is a prime, thumbs down if it isn't.

English: An ask: what characters are in this story?
A task: I will say the name of a character; thumbs up if they are in Red Riding Hood, thumbs down if they are not.

Science: An ask: which animal would live in the rainforest?
A task: I will say an animal; thumbs up if you would find them in the rainforest, thumbs down if you wouldn't.

PSHE: An ask: how can you be a good friend?
A task: I will say some actions; thumbs up if you think it is something a good friend does, thumbs down if you don't.

Mix it up

- Tell your partner why
- Walk and talk thumbs up/thumbs down and then discuss
- Write or draw your ideas on your whiteboard

TASK DON'T ASK: POPCORN

Up and down!

What is it?

Gather answers quickly by playing popcorn. Only works for one-word answers. Allows you to hear 'pops' of different answers across a range of pupils and increases to pace and energy.

Subject ideas

Maths: An ask: can you tell me a multiple of three?
A task: if I say your name, tell me a multiple of three.

English: An ask: can you tell me a noun?
A task: if I say your name, give me a noun.

Science: An ask: can anyone tell me the name of a plant?
A task: if I say your name, name a plant.

PSHE: An ask: what might you do when you're angry?
A task: if I say your name, tell me something people do when they are angry.

Geography: An ask: who can give me an example of human geography?
A task: if I say your name, tell me a type of human geography.

History: An ask: who can give me an example of a primary source?
A task: if I say your name, name a primary source.

Mix it up

- Can be done with a beach ball!
- Do word collection first
- Stand up when they say it

TASK DON'T ASK: FREEZE FRAME

Show don't tell

What is it?

Great for when you want to emphasise feelings or actions involved.

Subject ideas

English: An ask: how do you think the character felt?
A task: show me with your face how the character felt.
An ask: which one is the verb?
A task: show me the action of the verb.
An ask: what does this parenthesis tell us about how the character says it?
A task: say the line while doing the action.

PSHE: An ask: how would that make you feel?
A task: show me how that would make you feel.
An ask: she's finished her banana. What could she do with the skin to help the environment?
A task: show me what you'd do with the banana skin.

Geography: An ask: which way is north?
A task: stand up and point north.

History: An ask: what weapon was most popular in the Saxon times?
A task: show me what weapon you'd pick up in the Saxon times. Can you act out how you would use it?

PE: An ask: how do you start a race?
A task: show me what your starting race position looks like.

Mix it up

- Join up with a partner or a group to create a group frame
- Draw what you did
- Write what you did
- Describe your partner's actions

TASK DON'T ASK: FILL IN THE BLANKS

Why say it yourself when you can say it together?

What is it?

Have you ever asked a question when you really need a specific answer in order to move on or establish the same learning position for everyone? Fill in the blanks allows you to ensure you get the right answer and have everyone reviewing the learning together. Think about the key learning. Blank out some of the words. Read it and ask children to join in.

Metamorphic, Sedimentary and Igneous are all types of _____

Rocks

Example

Here is the information:

> Volcanoes erupt when molten rock, called magma, rises to the surface of the Earth and breaks through the crust. This can happen in a variety of ways, depending on the type of volcano and the composition of the magma. Some volcanoes erupt relatively gently, with lava flowing out of the crater and down the sides of the volcano. Other volcanoes erupt violently, with explosions that can send ash and rocks high into the atmosphere.

The ask might be:

1   What is molten rock called?
2   What does molten rock break through?
3   Where does the lava flow out?
4   What comes out in an explosion?

The task is:

Let's think about what we know about volcanoes! I will read this text twice. The first time you think in your heads what the missing words could be. The second time, if you know the missing words, join in!

Volcanoes erupt when molten rock, called _____, rises to the surface of the Earth and breaks through the _____. This can happen in a variety of ways, depending on the type of volcano and the composition of the magma. Some volcanoes _____ relatively gently, with lava flowing out of the crater and down the sides of the volcano. Other volcanoes erupt violently, with explosions that can send ____ and rocks high into the atmosphere.

Mix it up

- Have the bank of missing words on the bottom and give children thinking time
- Have children share the missing words to their partner first
- Incorporate movement and have children stand up when they fill in the blanks

TASK DON'T ASK: STICKY NOTE

Can't get enough of them

What is it?

Everyone loves a sticky note! Instead of asking children a question for one person to answer, ask them, get them to walk to their tables (hello movement my old friend), write it on a sticky note and come back. If children are already on tables. Have sticky notes on walls or on different surfaces to add extra excitement.

Subject ideas

Maths: An ask: if the answer is 12, what could the question be?
A task: if the answer is 12, what could the question be? Write an idea on a sticky note!

English: An ask: why do you think they should let Paddington stay with them?
A task: I think they should let Paddington stay with them because ... finish it on your sticky note.

Science: An ask: what do you know about insects?
A task: write one fact or draw one picture that is linked to insects on your sticky note.

Geography: An ask: what would you expect to see in a city?
A task: what would you expect to see in a city? Write or draw one idea on a sticky note.

History: An ask: what do you remember about Julius Caesar?
A task: what do you remember about Julius Caesar? Write one fact on a sticky note.

Mix it up

- Pick a selection of sticky notes to read out
- Ask children to go and collect a sticky note (that isn't their own) and share it with their partner
- Do an exhibition walk where children can view the different ideas
- Have children at tables pass their sticky notes round and read each other's

TASK DON'T ASK: SNOWBALL

Spoiler alert: it's pretty fun

Also seen in Chapter 20 on movement classroom essentials

What is it?

Sounds wild, but the children LOVE it. Snowball is when you give children a task that has legs. For example, how many nouns can you think of? Or name things you can do outdoors. Things you might see in Ancient Rome etc. Ask them to write as many as they can in a given timeframe (one min should suffice). Then collectively scrunch up the paper. Launch it. Collect a snowball and add it to it.

Subject ideas

Maths: An ask: if the answer is 12. What could the question be?
A task: give children a piece of paper with a number in the middle. Get them to write the question and then launch it. Collect another with a different number.

English: An ask: what images come to mind when you read this sentence?
A task: pick five to ten sentences with clear imagery. Hand them out (with some duplicates). Ask children to read the sentence and draw what imagery it depicts.

Geography: An ask: what have we learnt about London?
A task: draw or write anything you remember.

History: An ask: what might you see in Ancient Rome?
A task: write or draw as many things as you can that you might see in Ancient Rome.

PSHE: An ask: how can we show kindness?
A task: write or draw something that shows kindness.

Mix it up

- Give children templates like storyboards to fill in so it links collaboration, movement and engagement
- Have children work in pairs
- After two rounds ask children to use a highlighter or felt tip to circle or underline their favourite ideas
- Display flattened snowballs as a gallery

TASK DON'T ASK: TRACE IT!

A nice calming one

What is it?

Simply trace the answer on your palm or on the back of a partner!
Works best alongside number voting! The grounding nature of this task
supports a calming and community-focused atmosphere.

Subject ideas

English: An ask: which picture (1. Bus, 2. Dog, 3. Snake) has a b
sound?
A task: vote by tracing the number on their palm, the
carpet or a partner's back (consent dependent).

Science: An ask: which leaf is from autumn?
A task: vote by tracing the number on their palm, the
carpet or a partner's back (consent dependent).

History: An ask: which toy is from the past?
A task: vote by tracing the number on their palm, the
carpet or a partner's back (consent dependent).

Mix it up

- After the vote children can all say it at the same time
- See if they match their partner and discuss why or why not
- If there was another option, what could it be? Draw on your whiteboard
- Have children draw, write or discuss after tracing

TASK DON'T ASK: WRITE ON THE TABLES

It's me again!

What is it?

Split up the activity by asking children to reflect, respond or discuss on the table.

Subject ideas

Maths: An ask: what would the bar look like for this question?
A task: show three questions on the board. Ask children to pick one, go to their table and draw a bar for it. They can work independently or with a partner.

English: An ask: can you give me a sentence with a fronted adverbial?
A task: have three fronted adverbials on the board. Ask children to pick one and write a sentence for it on their table. They can work independently or with a partner.
An ask: what is the simile here?
A task: ask children to draw the simile on their table. They can work independently or with a partner.

Geography: An ask: what human geography did you spot in the video?
A task: ask children to draw an aspect of human geography they spotted on their table.

History: An ask: which sources are most reliable?
A task: ask children to draw or write a source that they deem to be most reliable on their table.

Mix it up

- Pair up with an exhibition walk to view answers
- Pair up with a walk and talk to discuss the task
- Ask children to switch seats and add to the table ideas (similar to snowball)

TASK DON'T ASK: A WRITTEN DEBATE

The pen does the talking!

What is it?

Instead of asking children their opinions and conducting a debate through hands up, try a written debate. Simply ask children to take turns writing their thoughts. Great to do on flip chart paper with different coloured pens so you can visibly see the debate!

I think zoos should be banned because they are cruel.

Zoos stop animals from becoming extinct.

Subject ideas

Asks that can be turned into this task:

PSHE: Should we ban social media for kids?
Should we have a digital detox day once a week?
Should we have pineapple on pizza?
Should children be able to vote?
Should we ban plastic?
Should we ban homework?
English: Is Julian a bad friend?
Was Goldilocks a bad person?
Should Robin Hood be captured?
Is the wolf really big and bad?

Mix it up

- Use bullet points or key words to begin with
- Have two sides of your classroom 'For and Against' with flipcharts stuck up for children to walk back and forth and annotate with other students

TASK DON'T ASK: STORYBOARD

What happens next?

What is it?

A great way to tap into creative and expression where everyone can get involved. It is basically 'what happens next'. Think about a comic strip. You show them the first part of the storyboard and they complete the next two (or more) in the sequence. They can do this on whiteboards, on a template or directly on tables.

Subject ideas

English: An ask: what do you think August (Wonder) will do next?
A task: draw what you think August will do next.

Geography: An ask: what is the first part of the water cycle?
A task: water vapour rises and collects in the sky as clouds. What happens next? Draw it on your whiteboard.

Science: An ask: how does pollination happen?
A task: insects are attracted to a flower by bright colours and strong smells. Draw what happens next.

History: An ask: how do you play the Ancient Maya game: pitz?
A task: the game starts with two teams and a ball. Draw what might happen next.

Mix it up

- Children can work with partners
- Children can annotate and colour to lead into a comic strip
- You could work in groups to act out children's storyboards
- You could add speech and thought bubbles
- Where appropriate they can be turned into playscripts

CHAPTER 22
G IS FOR GAME TIME

CLASSROOM ESSENTIALS

CRACK THE CODE

You tell me what to do

Age range: all ages

What is it?

Instead of telling children what they are learning, instead of telling children what their task is, show them visuals (of GIFs!) and get them to crack the code.

When can I use it?

This is a great strategy for replacing teacher-only instruction.

Why does it work?

Children are no longer the 'receivers'; they are the discoverers! This element of challenge and mission sparks immediate engagement! It also increases processing and comprehension.

Steps

1   Think about your teacher instruction.
2   Summarise the task or instruction in three to five images (depending on year group).
3   Invite children to crack the code with their partner!

Simplify

Use three images or fewer and focus on consistent daily tasks such as getting their coat, bottle and bag.

Challenge

You can extend *crack the code* to group or individual tasks. If you want children to do different activities you can set them on secret group missions!

BARRIER

A classic!

Age range: six+

What is it?

Children work in pairs; one child looks at an image and describes it to the other child. The child listening has to draw the image based on their partner's description.

When can I use it?

This is a great playful game for new topics. The image can be a book cover, an artefact, a historical painting, a landscape or ANY image linked to what you are learning about.

Why does it work?

Instead of showing an image, children are now exploring the details in a completely different playful context. Children are excited to work collaboratively and WANT to do the task.

Steps

1 Think about what you're learning about.
2 Pick a relevant image.
3 Play barrier!

Simplify

If you're just starting out with barrier, start with a simple image! We want our children to feel success. Don't start with the *Mona Lisa!*

Challenge

You can also play barrier in groups. It might be three children describing to three children. Or one child describing to a group of four. This extends that level of challenge.

PUZZLE

The OG game

Age range: all ages

What is it?

We know what a puzzle is! Here is the difference, this is a puzzle you have created based on the learning. No, I am not talking about getting the laminator out. Simply take a text or an image, snip it up and give it to children in groups.

When can I use it?

Honestly, any lesson!
Maths ideas might include snipping up the questions and the answers, a symmetrical image, a pattern, a graph.
English ideas might be: snipping up a text for comprehension, a front cover of a book, grammar worksheets, illustrations linked to a writing stimulus.
The possibilities are endless.

Why does it work?

Similar to barrier; instead of just showing them an image, they are now uncovering their learning in a gamified approach.

Steps

1   Think about what you're learning about.
2   Pick a relevant image or text.
3   Snip it up.
4   Put it in a paperclip or envelope.
5   Ask children to uncover the missing image/text.

Simplify

Just focus on images! Limit how many puzzle pieces.

Challenge

Include text too and increase the number of puzzle pieces.

BOARD GAME: SNAKES AND LADDERS

Crowd pleaser!

Age range: all ages

What is it?

Board games are naturally fun and collaborative. We can easily take the blueprint of a board game and remix it to our learning focus.

When can I use it?

This game of luck and unpredictability is perfect for engaging pupils. Adding questions in allows children to seamlessly learn through play.

Why does it work?

This is best for any lessons where you want to consolidate learning.

Steps

1   Identify key learning children have covered.
2   Separate into key questions.
3   Input on a snakes and ladders template.
4   Invite your children to play in pairs or groups.

Simplify

Play in teacher-focused groups or as a whole class by splitting the class into groups.

Challenge

Have children create their own snakes and ladders games by giving them a template (there are lots available on Canva). Children can add questions linked to the learning on the squares and then swap with another pair to play their version!

BOARD GAME: THREE IN A ROW

Grids at the ready!

Age range: all ages

What is it?

Start with your three in a row grid. This can be used for so many different parts of your lesson. Here are some ideas.

1   Fill the grid with images; they have to get three in a row by identifying the sounds.
2   Slot in words and they need to use them in a sentence.
3   Put numbers in and they need to create a number sentence for it.
4   Use animals; they have to outline the food chain.
5   Add material images and they need to name three things made from it.

The goal is still the same, who can get three in a row first?

When can I use it?

A great game for consolidating!

Why does it work?

It is low risk! It doesn't feel like a test, it feels fun and children will want to play!

Steps

1   Identify key learning children have covered.
2   Separate six images, questions, words or prompts.
3   Input on a three by three grid (or just do one on paper and photocopy!).
4   Invite your children to play in pairs or groups.

Simplify

Play in teacher-focused groups or as a whole class by splitting the class into groups.

Challenge

Liz from playfullearninggames.co.uk shares some incredible insights on how to adapt further for older learners. Instead of just crossing off, add another layer of learning. Liz shows a grid with different words. There are then sticky notes with word classes. Not only do children have to get three in a row but they need to match up the word with the appropriate word class. Her website is well worth checking out.

STICKY NOTE GAMES

GAME

A resource we always have in the drawer!

Age range: all ages

What is it?

The basics of this game is a question and answer. On one coloured sticky note add the questions, on another add the answers. You could do this in groups and have the answers on one side and the questions on the other so there is some added movement too! You could also have it as a scavenger hunt around the room or outside.

When can I use it?

Another great game for consolidating instead of a ... worksheet.

Why does it work?

There is a quest element involved here that supports motivation. The hands-on style is supportive for that whole-body learning.

Steps

1   Identify key learning children have covered.
2   Separate into questions and answers on different coloured sticky notes.
3   Put children into groups or pairs to match up.

Simplify

Play in teacher-focused groups.
You could also do one big class game with 15 answers and 15 questions. Scrunch up the sticky notes and hand them out. Children need to find their match.

Challenge

Add another element by numbering the sticky notes and adding a die! Children take turns to roll the die, find the relevant sticky note and then the matching answer!

Liz from playfullearninggames.co.uk shares a brilliant example for multiplication. She arranges half of the sticky notes (say the answers) to create a board game route. Children roll the die and work through the board game; when they land on the answer they need to find the sticky note question that matches it!

TUFF TRAY GAMES

Long live the tuff tray

Age range: all ages

What is it?

The concept of a tuff tray activity is to add a playful prompt with manipulatives to explore. However, this doesn't just have to stay in the Early Years. It doesn't mean you need a tray, you could easily use desks.

When can I use it?

A great playful game for exploring learning. Here are some ideas.

1   Give children perimeter or area goals to create with Lego®.
2   Give children a selection of books to find adjectives/nouns or specific punctuation.
3   Explore capacity with a range of containers.
4   Use a deck of cards to create number sentences.
5   Use cubes to show fractions.
6   Have large maps on tables, atlases with small world animals to match up.

Why does it work?

Manipulatives provide a concrete, tactile way for students to interact with abstract concepts. This hands-on approach makes learning more engaging and memorable.

Steps

1   Identify key learning to explore.
2   Identify manipulatives linked to the learning.
3   Provide a prompt and an opportunity for children to explore on tables.

Simplify

Have a tuff tray set up for the week that children can explore in groups each lesson.

Challenge

Give children manipulatives – i.e. sticky notes, blocks, counters etc. – and ask them to come up with their own provocations linked to the learning!

FLOWER

Hangman was a bit weird, wasn't it?

Age range: six+

What is it?

Basically hangman, but not depressing. Instead of creating a hangman, create a flower. Children think of a word linked to the learning and play!

When can I use it?

Perfect for a starter or a finishing task.

Why does it work?

It is simple, low resource and fast-paced.

Steps

1   Ask children to think of as many words as they can linked to the lesson and make a 'secret' list on paper.
2   Invite children to play FLOWER using their key words.
3   Children can give clues linked to the word.

Simplify

Play as a class for children who are still learning to read and write. Focus on the specific sounds.

Challenge

Team flower!
Similar to charades, children play in teams. They have a set time to guess the word in. You can decide a limit on how many clues they are allowed to give.

BINGO

Let's bring it back!

Age range: all ages

What is it?

Have a set of words, images, numbers (or anything really) on a grid. Use the same data but change the order. You decide what BINGO is. It might be the first person to get three, four or five in a row. Don't call out the words/numbers/images; instead give clues for children to solve and then see if they have the answer.

When can I use it?

A great game for exploring or consolidating the learning in any subject.

Why does it work?

Who doesn't like the thrill of finding the last item on your list, jumping up and shouting you won? Everyone can play the game together, regardless of level.

Steps

1   Identify key learning children have covered.
2   Identify key words/pictures or numbers.
3   Organise on a grid and create 15 different combinations.
4   Print one and cut it up for each round.

Simplify

Have children play in partners so they can collaboratively support each other and remove the pressure.
Replace words with pictures.

Challenge

When someone has five squares in a row, make them do something with the five squares (e.g. use the words in a sentence, create a number sentence). If they aren't sure, they can ask their class for ideas – leaning back on collaboration.

Children can volunteer to select and give a clue to the class.

FOUR PICTURES, ONE WORD

Curiosity forever!

Age range: all ages

What is it?

Show children four pictures linked to the learning and get them to figure out what they think they are learning about.

When can I use it?

A fun replacement for the learning objective walk through.

Why does it work?

It taps into that glorious natural curiosity when children want to find the answer.

Steps

1   Identify your learning objective.
2   Search the topic in Canva or Google.
3   Pick four images.
4   Ask children what they are learning about!

Simplify

Start with three pictures to avoid cognitive overload.

Challenge

Once children find the word – i.e. fractions – you could have a set of another four images to narrow down that learning objective: 'identify' the three pictures that show 'a half'.

Tell half the class the learning objective and have the other half face away from the board. They need to draw four images on their whiteboard that summarise that objective for their partner to guess.

WHICH ONE DOESN'T BELONG?

Perfect for talkers!

Age range: all ages

What is it?

Show children a series of images of words linked to the learning with one that doesn't quite belong. They need to decide which one it is. Here are some examples.

1   Descriptions of a character.
2   Words with the same sound.
3   Square numbers.
4   Abstract nouns.

It really fits in with anything you're learning.

When can I use it?

A great starter for any lesson. You could also use it within the teacher input to formatively assess the learning.

Why does it work?

It feels safe and the hint of game show element supports children to confidently have a guess.

Steps

1   Identify the key learning you want to consolidate or assess.
2   Pick four words/images or numbers ensuring one or more could be considered the odd one out.
3   Ask children to find the odd one out and explain why.

Simplify

Work in partners to agree and answer to support confidence and dialogue.
Start with four elements and then expand.

Challenge

Even better if there can be multiple odd ones out. You can do this with words, pictures or numbers.
2, 8, 22, 7
Is it 22 because it is the only one with two digits?
7 as it is the only odd one?

IMAGINATION WORKOUT

Creative exploration time

Age range: all ages

What is it?

Create a squiggle of some sort. Yes, I said squiggle! A mark, a dot, a dash, a starting point. After the teacher-led input, ask children 'How do you think this is linked to the learning?' Children may turn it into a drawing, word (or even word art) to reflect something they have learnt.

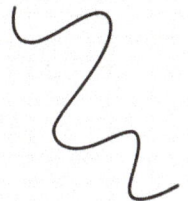

When can I use it?

After any kind of input. Whether they have read a story, watched a video, listened to you – get your squiggle on!

Why does it work?

It provides children with a playful opportunity to reflect on their learning in a way that is unique to them! The creative 'squiggle' element takes the pressure off!

Steps

1   Deliver the key learning in your chosen format.
2   Draw a squiggle (I'm making squiggle happen!).
3   Photocopy the squiggle.
4   Tell children it is part of a drawing or word linked to the learning.
5   Ask children to complete the squiggle!

Simplify

Have children work in pairs.

Challenge

Storyboard it! Have three to five boxes with different squiggles for children to recreate a sequence of learning.

HEADS UP

The game that lives on!

Age range: all ages

What is it?

I remember playing a version of this at my aunty's New Year party in the late 90s! Ten years ago it was adapted to an app (of course). But let's bring it to the classroom. Super-easy: you have a word on your head that you can't see. Your partner or group has to describe it to you. You can use sticky notes, but I would recommend making some card headbands as the sticky note is more likely to stay on and that way you have an excuse to play again!

When can I use it?

To consolidate or review learning. Great as an oracy-focused task before writing too!

Why does it work?

Who am I? What am I? The curiosity and intrigue of the game is so compelling. The collaborative element taps into our human need for connection as well and joy.

Steps

1   Identify key learning from your lesson/topic.
2   Create a collection of related words or pictures.
3   Have children blindly pick and stick on their headband.
4   Children need to take turns asking questions and describing to each other.

Simplify

Use pictures! It might be the same pictures throughout the week linked to your learning – for example, Goldilocks and the Three Bears. Model it during carpet time and then have the headbands as part of your continuous provision for children to play together.

Challenge

Have children write key words linked to the learning. Collect them and hand them out for them!

You can also get children to play in teams, similar to Pictionary®, where their team needs to describe it to them in a given timeframe to get a point.

PICTIONARY

Need I say more?

Age range: six+

What is it?

Have keywords linked to the learning. Children work in teams. They pick a word and have to draw it for their team to guess within a timeframe.

When can I use it?

You could use it as a pre-teach to include words that will be linked to the lesson. For example, if you are looking at Viking ships you might want to include speedboat, kayak, cruise ship, pedalo etc. to start developing that schema of vehicles.

You can also use it as a way to review or consolidate learning. Once children have learnt about something they can then draw it and process it in a different way. Great for oracy too!

Why does it work?

The brain's reward system is activated when players successfully guess or communicate effectively, leading to positive emotions and increased motivation.

Steps

1   Identify the key words linked to the learning.
2   Organise children into Pictionary teams.
3   Children to take turns blindly picking a word and drawing it for their team to guess.

Simplify

Play as a whole class first. This will support children to understand the structure of the game. You could pick a word and draw and then children could volunteer to do the same.

Challenge

Have children generate the words themselves and then mix them up and distribute them across the class.

TABOO

Use your words

Age range: six+

What is it?

An oracy game! Children need to describe a word but they have a set of 'taboo' words they are not allowed to say.

When can I use it?

Great as a starter, a finishing task or a strategy to review or consolidate key learning.

Why does it work?

It taps into that gamification element of adding extra hurdles.

Steps

1   Think about keywords linked to the learning.
2   Create a template with the word at the top and two to five words they cannot say.
3   Have children work in pairs. Partner A faces away from the board and Partner B looks at the board.
4   On the board is the word to describe and the taboo words they are not allowed to use!
5   Once confident, print out cards for children to blindly select in partners or groups.

Simplify

Start with only two to three taboo words!
I would also recommend using as a whole class first. You can ask a volunteer to come to the front and sit with their back to the whiteboard. Display the word and the taboo words. The class need to put their hand up to explain to the 'guesser'.

Challenge

Have children develop their own taboo cards based on the learning or topic and play them every lesson!

CATEGORIES

Age range: five+

What is it?

Create categories and come up with words linked to the learning and each category. The easiest one is the alphabet! You could also do word classes and you could get creative with more discussion-focused categories such as 'The most significant part', 'An area I want to know more about' etc.

When can I use it?

To introduce a topic or review/consolidate a piece of learning.

Why does it work?

The game requires players to think quickly and creatively! The mental (but appropriate) challenge is often stimulating and enjoyable.

Steps

1 Choose your categories and write on the board or scrap paper.
2 Pick your chosen topic.
3 Choose to do it timed or not.
4 Choose to do partners, groups or independent.
5 Play categories!

Simplify

Link to your sounds of the week. For example, if you have learnt the sounds m, a, s, d, t as a class, try and match your sounds to your topics.
What parts of the body start with these sounds?
What family members start with these sounds?

Challenge

Give children a timeframe to complete as many categories as possible with their partner.

CHATTERBOX

Or do you call them fortune tellers?

Age range: six+

What is it?

Your children will be so excited to explore your learning if it is in the form of a chatterbox. A chatterbox (or fortune teller) is a papercraft/origami that supports children to ask different questions and build fun discussions around a topic.

When can I use it?

Perfect for reviewing or consolidating learning.

Why does it work?

Busy hands? Yes please! Design your own? We love autonomy! Q & A without the snoring part? Yep, that too!

Steps

1   Decide on the key topic or learning.
2   Ask children to identify key questions linked to the learning that they can include in their chatterbox.
3   Print a chatterbox template (easy to find online).
4   Children can design.
5   Play chatterboxes.

Simplify

Give children a list of possible discussion prompts or questions for children to include.

Challenge

Give children different topics to explore to support more comprehensive discussions. For example, each table could focus on a particular character, material, country, artefact etc.

PLAY-DOUGH

Getting squidgy with it

Age range: all ages

What is it?

Give children play-dough to recreate their learning. That's it!

When can I use it?

During any time you want children to explore or review their learning.

Why does it work?

The tactile element is super-calming and enjoyable. The process of open creation provides an engaging provocation for pupils that they want to take part in.

Steps

1   Think about the key learning.
2   Ask children to recreate something they have learnt with play-dough.
3   Give children the opportunity to share what they have created with their partner or group.

Simplify

Some children may find the openness of this playful game a challenge. Children can create in partners to support this. You can also create a list of keywords or ideas before they start.

Challenge

Give children a more specific task in groups. For example, recreate the last chapter with as many details as you can. Or recreate the parts of a plant.

GAME SHOW

Cue the music

Age range: all ages

What is it?

Recreate a classic game show in your classroom. Simply identify key questions linked to the topic. Ask them in a game show style by giving children multiple choices as well as 'life lines' like phone a friend. Add a timer to make it fast-paced!

When can I use it?

Whenever you need to review or consolidate key learning.

Why does it work?

The gamification element of getting to the next round keeps children gripped!

Steps

1   Identify the key learning.
2   Establish five to ten questions.
3   Create slides with multiple choices.
4   Add a timer if children are ready!
5   Don't forget to add some theatrics!

Simplify

Do the game show as a whole class and have children vote with their body or fingers which is the correct answer. Take away the timer if your children are at the beginning stage!

Challenge

Have children create their own simple game show in groups to deliver to each other. This can simply include question cards, a timer and life lines!

YOU SUNK MY BATTLESHIP!

It's retro and we love it

Age range: seven+

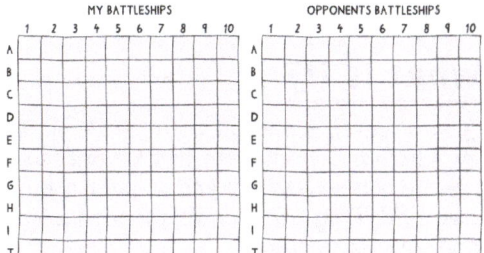

What is it?

Print off battleship grids (easy to find online). You can put them in pocket wallets so you can reuse again and again. Identify the keywords/spelling list as a class. Children then plot them into their grid vertically, horizontally or diagonally. They need to take turns saying grid references. If they get a letter their partner needs to say which letter so they can problem-solve where the rest of the word is!

When can I use it?

Perfect for practising spelling or key vocabulary.

Why does it work?

There's a perfect mixture of luck and strategy!

Steps

1   Identify the keywords or spelling list.
2   Children input into their grids.
3   Take turns suggesting grid references.
4   If they get a letter they have to reveal which one they hit!
5   Continue until all words are found!

Simplify

Compete in groups of four, with children playing with their partner. This will support them with the strategy!

Challenge

Instead of telling them the letter they've revealed, they can give a clue about the word – i.e. it's an adjective.

WORDSEARCH

Get plotting!

Age range: seven+

What is it?

A wordsearch is always a winner. A blank wordsearch is even better. Give children blank word searches to choose their list of keywords linked to the learning and input into their grid. They can then fill the blanks with letters and try and solve each other's.

When can I use it?

Great as a starter or a finishing task!

Why does it work?

The idea that other children have to solve it is exciting! It brings that purpose element into the playful game.

r	e	a	d	P	u	y	s
g	i	f	b	v	e	j	n
i	P	n	o	w	b	n	o
s	c	h	o	o	l	P	e
y	w	l	k	r	f	g	t
h	o	m	e	k	s	t	i
t	i	m	e	a	z	m	r
h	c	q	u	d	r	a	w

1. read   4. draw   7. time
2. book   5. pen   8. school
3. write   6. work   9. home

Steps

1 Identify the keywords for the learning or topic.
2 Give children blank grids.
3 Have children create their wordsearch.
4 Swap with other children to play.

Simplify

Try creating with partners instead of independently.

Challenge

Put the wordsearches in pocket wallets. That way you can hand them out each lesson as an engaging starter.

TOP TRUMPS

It's all in the cards!

Age range: seven+

What is it?

The concept of top trumps is having cards linked to a topic such as animals or dinosaurs. All cards in the deck have the same categories. This might be danger rating, speed, unique factor etc. You can recreate this with your topic. For example, characters in your core text could have the categories friend rating, brave rating etc. Materials in science might have sustainability factor, versatility etc. Historical figures might have loyalty, innovation etc. Children can play to explore the topic in an oracy-focused, playful way.

When can I use it?

This could be a class project that they add to each lesson. Or it could be something you create and children play every lesson – adding to their subject knowledge and debates!

Why does it work?

The opportunity for debate! Top trumps allows you to argue your answer and justify your point. This entices children to want to play!

Steps

1   Identify the learning topic and different card ideas.
2   Identify the criteria for each card.
3   Either create the cards or have children create them each lesson.
4   Play top trumps!

Simplify

Create the cards to use in every lesson!

Challenge

Have children create a new set of cards each lesson to add to the pack.

TREASURE HUNT/ SCAVENGER HUNT

Dial up that question and answer

Age range: all ages

What is it?

A collaborative to 'hunt' to find the answers. You can simplify or extend this to your class.

When can I use it?

A great game for getting children to enthusiastically focus on the learning.

Why does it work?

The novelty, the unpredictability and rush of a hunt all adds to the engagement!

Steps

1   Identify key areas of learning you want children to explore or review.
2   Plant text/images or words around the room or area.
3   Create a grid of certain things they need to find. You can make this explicit or ambiguous by giving clues.
4   Children need to find them and cross them off the grid.

Simplify

Focus on the scavenger hunt element. Can you find something beginning with the 'm' sound? Can you find something made of wood? This works best in focus groups so children can orally tell or show you what they have found.

Challenge

Give children riddles that lead to certain answers or locations which they then need to find. At each location have a new riddle waiting for them!

MASKING TAPE GAMES

GAME

Let's make it big!

Age range: all ages

What is it?

Another great concept from Liz from playfullearninggames. co.uk. Whether it is a giant wordsearch with magnetic letters, calculating the perimeter, creating a number square, place value grid, giant 'flower', squares for number sentences, grid references, timeline, giant noughts and crosses ... whatever you're doing make it big!

When can I use it?

Any task that requires a pictorial model of some sort, make it a masking tape one!

Why does it work?

It feels more creative and interesting to do things on a bigger scale!

Steps

1   Identify the key learning and pictorial models involved.
2   Give children masking tape in groups.
3   Invite children to create the pictorial model in groups.
4   Give children a set of questions to explore and investigate using the giant pictorial scaffold.

Simplify

Create the scaffold for children with an invitation to play – for example, a giant number sentence with big numbers.

Challenge

Invite children to create their own props or questions linked to their pictorial model. Have children swap groups and solve the problems presented.

STORYTELLING STRATEGY 'I WONDER ...'

Let's strip it back

Age range: all ages

What is it?

The most simple strategy in this collection. Instead of telling children the task, entice them with an 'I wonder ...'

I wonder...

'I wonder who can come up with the craziest ingredients in their recipe.'

'I wonder who will learn something completely new from this page.'

'I wonder if your opinion will change about the character.'

'I wonder if you will feel anything bumpy today!'

When can I use it?

To introduce a task!

Why does it work?

Yes. It is simple. But the learning doesn't seem like a task they have to complete any more because ... they just do. It feels like a challenge, it feels like an invitation, it feels like a game!

Steps

1   Think about the task you are introducing. Think about how you could add a challenge to it.
2   Pitch your 'I wonder' with excitement!

Note: Your 'I wonder' shouldn't focus on attainment or competition – i.e. 'I wonder who will write the most' – as this feels like it is a win or a fail.

Simplify

Start with tasks that don't require evidence. This way when children do it and share with you, they also feel that sense of community and dopamine. That becomes the magic, not the outcome.

Challenge

Invite your children to wonder too! What do you wonder about this task?

OBSTACLE COURSE

Mind the gap

Age range: all ages

What is it?

What if your question and answer was an obstacle course? Seriously. Set up three or four different obstacle courses outside or in a hall. Whatever you have (cones, skipping rope, benches etc.). Have children work in pairs going through them. But there are also questions along the way they have to answer in order to move forward.

When can I use it?

To review or consolidate learning.

Why does it work?

The element of risk, the teamwork, the achievement of getting through it! Not to mention, the creative way to explore key learning.

Steps

1   Identify key questions linked to the learning (four to five per obstacle course).
2   Set up three to four obstacle courses outside or in a hall.
3   Split children into groups.
4   Have pairs work through the obstacle course together answering questions along the way.

Simplify

Identify the 'questioner' in each obstacle course. This might be a child who is less confident with the learning. They then get to hear the answers multiple times in a non-threatening way.

Challenge

Have children create their own obstacle course and questions for other groups to trial!

Add a blindfold to further support oracy and teamwork.

WHO ARE YA?

And action!

Age range: six+

What is it?

Have children approach a task 'in role' – i.e. you are now:
- reporters
- investigators
- jewel thieves!
- presenters
- content creators.

When can I use it?

Whenever it suits a task! I remember when I was training to be a teacher, every lesson I put children in a different role to 'solve' or 'play out'
a task.

Why does it work?

It taps into playful purpose. There is a problem to solve! Ultimately, children are playing 'pretend' which helps children develop cognitive skills, such as memory, attention and language. They can practise remembering details, following instructions and expressing themselves verbally.

Steps

1   Identify the key learning.
2   Put it into a context.
3   'Deliver' it to children as that context.
4   Use that same language: 'As reporters you need to ...'

Simplify

Have the whole class doing the same context to strengthen the language and understanding.

Challenge

Have children play out different roles. For example, in a court you can have the jury, defence, prosecutors etc. Or perhaps a House of Commons with different political parties present.

GRAB A BALL

Show me you're ready!

Age range: all ages

What is it?

Grab a beach ball and incorporate it into your game. Give me a noun, a word beginning with m, something you'd see in Victorian England, a city in the UK ... The list goes on!

When can I use it?

Starters or the end of a lesson – fast-paced question and answer.

Why does it work?

It makes it playful and high energy!

Steps

1   Think of a leading question with multiple answers.
2   Present the question to your class.
3   Give them thinking time (or a partner talk).
4   Throw and answer.

Simplify

Roll it to each other in a circle to support that eye-hand coordination (and save furniture!).

Challenge

Have children come up with their own questions each lesson on sticky notes and stick them on the ball.

ENVELOPE CHALLENGE

Why does this always work?!

Age range: six+

What is it?

Dissect your lesson into challenges or a set of tasks. Put each one in an envelope and have children solve them in their group. For example:

1   find an adverb in this story;
2   use this adverb in a sentence;
3   think of an adverb beginning with f;
4   look at this picture and come up with three appropriate adverbs;
5   draw this adverb.

Obviously, that is just with adverbs! But you can do it with so many different types of learning.

When can I use it?

Your learning task.

Why does it work?

The envelope. It's the envelope. It makes it secretive, challenging and has a mysterious element that children will want to know more about!

Steps

1   Identify the key learning.
2   Split it into four to six mini tasks.
3   Put these into envelopes.
4   Have children solve each task and then pass on the envelope.

Simplify

Start with a focus group.

Challenge

Add a timer to each task!

Have children create their own tasks linked to the learning to invite other groups to solve.

GRAB A DECK

Got any cards lying around?

Age range: six+

What is it?

A deck of cards can be used for so many maths games! You can use a traditional deck or a UNO® deck.

- Fractions
- Put them in a place value grid (maybe that masking tape one!)
- What number am I? (did you save those headbands?)
- Number sentences

When can I use it?

So many maths opportunities!

Why does it work?

It adds a real-life context and prop to the lesson. It supports hands-on learning and, as cards are associated with games, it FEELS like you're playing.

Steps

1   Identify the key maths learning.
2   Create a scaffold (maybe with the masking tape).
3   Use the cards to explore questions.

Simplify

Start with a focus group.

Challenge

Have children create their own questions for other groups to solve.

Please see **References** section for links to specific playfullearning.co.uk resources.

CHAPTER 23
I IS FOR INTRINSIC MOTIVATION

CLASSROOM ESSENTIALS

PATHWAYS

Making learning visible

Age range: all ages

What is it?

Learning pathways™ is an approach, created by the Good Morning Club (TGMC, tgmc.uk), that supports you and your class to set goals visually and effectively. It supports cognitive load by chunking learning into three or four 'stops'. It complements growth mindset as all goals are presented as a journey with the likelihood of coming across obstacles. Children are expected to face obstacles, and the process includes problem-solving and 'bridging' that challenge together.

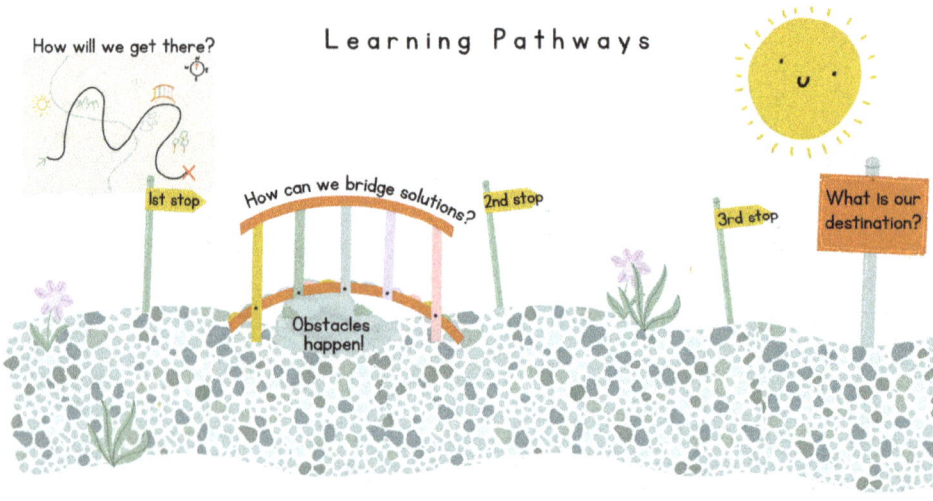

When can I use it?

Learning pathways were originally used to replace whole-class rewards. Instead of using extrinsic rewards and punitive consequences to condition behaviour, what if we taught through enhancing emotional and social skills? Learning pathways can also be used for any type of learning, whether it is writing a story, solving a maths problem or conducting an investigation.

Why does it work?

It works because it makes learning visible. When children see their progress visually on the pathways it supports that element of mastery! Pedagogically, it taps into growth mindset, cognitive load and connection.

Steps

1   Identify the destination (goal).
2   Identify the stops (to achieve the goal).
3   Identify obstacles (challenges) as and when they happen.
4   Bridge solutions to the obstacles.
5   Recognise the journey and how far children have come.

Simplify

Have one clear destination for the week, which you continue to work towards, and use the map to develop children's toolkit. You may want to have a physical 'map' area where children can get things that will support them to meet that destination – for example, word mats, sound buttons, manipulatives etc.

Challenge

Older children can set their own pathways on whiteboards, deciding their own stops and further developing their mastery.

CHECKLISTS

Everyone loves to tick things off

Age range: all ages

What is it?

I don't need to tell you, right? You're an educator. You basically invented checklists. But in case someone else picks up this book, it is a list of things to do that you can tick off.

When can I use it?

Whenever there is something to do, so in school? ALL THE TIME. It could be starting the task, for example:

- date
- title
- margin.

Or it could be the task:

- one digit per square
- add the ones first
- add the tens
- write the total.

Why does it work?

It works because when we tick something off it gives us a boost of dopamine. From a mastery perspective, it allows us to visually see what we have achieved. This makes us more engaged and invested to tick them all off!

Steps

1 Break down a task into three to five micro tasks.
2 Create the checklist.
3 Tick off as a class once complete.

Note: Any more than five will be cognitive overload.

Simplify

Make it completely visual with known visuals – i.e. collect my coat, bag and water bottle. You can also use sound buttons to support decoding of appropriate words.

Challenge

Once children are confident with class checklists you can move on to individual checklists. Older children will also be able to create their own checklists based on what they think their steps are.

MARKING KEYS

How do I know if I am doing well?

Age range: six+

What is it?

A marking key is when you connect symbols to parts of the success criteria. There are many ways to use this to support mastery, but the main concept is that children can see how successful they are based on the marking key symbols on their work. It also enables them to visibly see which areas they can improve and therefore develop further.

24.5.17 I am learning to write a free verse poem		Teacher check	Marking key
Success Criteria I will know I have been successful when…			
I can generate adjectives to describe a rainforest			A
I can build a sentence to describe a rainforest			✓
I can use capital letters at the start of each line			✱
I can use 2 adjectives in 1 sentence			+
I	GG	TA	Teacher

When can I use it?

Personally, I found that marking keys worked really well for writing. Which is really helpful because it can be tricky to unpick writing and make feedback super-explicit.

Why does it work?

It works because it provides instant and visual feedback. This allows children to see their current strengths and next steps. It also creates a constructive dialogue between the educator and pupil about their progress. When children can see and talk about how they are meeting a task, it drives them further!

Steps

1   Create your success criteria (as normal).
2   Create a marking key that matches each step.
3   Use the marking key to mark children's writing.

Note: Live marking is even better for this!

Simplify

Have one that you focus on and gradually increase – for example, finger spaces.

Challenge

Once children are confident with marking keys you can ask them to mark their own work using the symbols before you check it. You can also provide 'stop and mark' times within writing lessons. This is brilliant for mastery as it enables children to stop and reflect on what they have achieved so far.

WHICH STEP?

Get children moving

Age range: five+

What is it?

The Resilience Steps™ are a TGMC concept that creates an opportunity for children to unpick what type of attitude and mindset they are experiencing.

I did it!

I will do it!

I can do it!

I'll try to do it.

How do I do it?

I want to do it.

I can't do it!

I won't do it!

When can I use it?

The resilience steps are the perfect habitual strategy to support metacognition, reflection and regulation. The more you use it, the more children will strengthen these skills. It shouldn't just be reserved for when children are disengaged. Ask children little and often 'Which step are you on right now?'

Why does it work?

This approach is helpful as it enables you and the child to problem-solve what strategies they can use to move them up the staircase. From a mastery perspective, children can visually experience themselves progressing through the lesson and up the steps, adding fuel to their engagement!

Steps

1   Teach the steps and what each one might feel like and what strategies we could use on each step.
2   Display the steps in your classroom or even on tables.
3   Ask children 'What step are you on?'
4   Reflect with children 'Which step did you get to?'

Simplify

Try doing it as a whole class and link it in with other strategies such as learning pathways to strengthen that understanding.

Challenge

For children who need extra support to see their progress, use resilience steps each lesson. They can annotate on a laminated copy or a copy in a plastic wallet. They could have a laminated one stuck to their whiteboard or desk. Seeing their progress often will support that drive of mastery.

WIN SCRIPTS

Make your feedback count

Age range: all ages

What is it?

WIN scripts were created by Ginny Lalieu within TGMC. They are an alternative way to praise children which provide specific feedback to support mastery. We love an 'amazing' or a 'fantastic', but when it comes to learning, children need to know more in order to repeat that success again.

W – witness (describe what you see or saw)
I – invite (encourage them to share their experience and perspective)
N – name (name the skill or character trait)

For example, instead of saying 'Good job' for finishing their work we can say:
'Wow, I noticed you finished all of your work; how does it feel? That is what I call perseverance!'

INTRINSIC

When can I use it?

If a child has achieved something, use it! You don't have to complete abandon the classic 'Good job', but sprinkling in some WIN scripts makes a big difference!

Why does it work?

It works because children are given a much clearer understanding of what they did well so they can repeat it again. It is also effective because children are given an opportunity to reflect and process their achievement which increases the likelihood of it going into their long-term memory.

Steps

1   Witness
    I can see you are ...
    I noticed ...
    Thank you for ...
2   Invite
    How does it feel?

What helped?
Was it tricky?
3   Name
    That's what I call ...
    I call that ...
    Great example of ...

Simplify

If scripts aren't your thing, just remember to ask them about their success before you jump in with how proud you are. For younger learners you might have a focus such as collaboration. You and your team can focus on collaboration feedback and praise. This will support the language network of your children.

Challenge

When children feel particularly proud you may want to mark that moment. Writing it in a journal or taking a photo can support children to see their progress and further drive that mastery.

MICRO CHOICES

What can they control?

Age range: all ages

What is it?

Handing over control to our children can feel like an absolute no no. But if we know autonomy is important, micro choices are a great way to incorporate choice in every lesson. Micro choices are just that. Tiny everyday choices children can make.

INTRINSIC

When can I use it?

Hopefully, you can use micro choices in every single lesson!

Why does it work?

Micro choices enable children to have and actively feel a sense of autonomy which taps into their intrinsic motivation.

Steps

1   Can children choose if they work alone or with a friend?
2   Can children choose what equipment/stationery they use?
3   Can children choose what order they do tasks in?

Simplify

Start with one micro choice you will have each lesson. Maybe they can choose whether they do the task by themselves or with the person next to them.

Challenge

Cross-reference micro choices with checklists and/or learning pathways. That will enable reflection and metacognition. You can ask children: 'Since making that choice have you ticked anything else off?/moved closer to your goal?' Combining that mastery and autonomy is a powerful mix!

LEARNING WISH

What do I actually want to learn?

Age range: all ages

What is it?

Who remembers KWL grids? This is basically the same concept but a bit more DRIVEN, shall we say. KWL grids are when children write what they:

- **K**now
- **W**ant to know

And have

- **L**earnt within a topic.

A learning wish is when you present children with the topic and ask them what they would like it to include. For example, if you are doing Ancient Rome children can write their learning wishes such as: weapons, wars, food, fashion etc. You then actually use their learning wishes within your planning.

When can I use it?

Works best for topic-based subjects.

Why does it work?

Children don't feel like they are being delivered a list of things to remember. They now feel like they are equal partners in the curriculum and want to learn about it.

Steps

1   Pick an appropriate topic.
2   Give children a summary and maybe some visuals – a story or a video – to introduce that topic.
3   Ask children what they would like to learn about.
4   Get them to write their learning wishes.
5   Highlight the learning wish when it comes up in lessons!

Simplify

Some children may struggle with autonomy at first so you can use choice boards and ask them what they are most interested in. You could also do a vote and then choose the most voted.

Challenge

For your older children you will be able to do this in more lessons and give children the resources – i.e. texts or tablets – to help them retrieve the information.

CLASSROOM AUTONOMY

How will we learn?

Age range: six+

What is it?

A key choice we can utilise in the classroom is where children work. This links back to our flexible sitting. Do they have to do this particular learning in a chair or are there options?

When can I use it?

Any lessons that aren't prescribed to a specific sitting position. For example, you will want children in chairs for handwriting!

Why does it work?

When children are comfortable and when children can choose their preferences for comfortability, we limit barriers to engagement.

Steps

1   Can they sit on the floor?
2   Can they lay on the floor?
3   Can they stand at their desk?
4   Can you stick it on the wall, and they work from there?

Simplify

Start with just two options and expand further.

Challenge

Cross-reference sitting choices with checklists and/or learning pathways that will enable reflection and metacognition. You can ask children: 'Since making that choice have you ticked anything else off?/moved closer to your goal?' Combining that mastery and autonomy is a powerful mix!

GENIUS HOUR

No rulebook

Age range: six+

What is it?

A genius hour is an educational concept that encourages creativity and intrinsic learning in students by allowing them to choose what they learn and how they learn it. Teachers provide an hour in class each week for students to focus on their chosen topic and work on a specific project using that subject. I know it sounds a bit wild but so many schools do *golden time* every week. Instead of a contingent reward time, let children pursue a project or an idea every week!

When can I use it?

If your curriculum allows it, once a week!

Why does it work?

It instils that love of learning and encourages children to purse their passions. It also enables you to see if you can weave any of their projects into your current curriculum.

Steps

1   Set aside an hour each week.
2   Provide tablets if you can, non-fiction texts if not.
3   Encourage children to bring projects or activities in like board games or cardboard.
4   Enjoy!

Simplify

Continuous provision is genius hour every hour!

Challenge

This can also extend into a time where children teach each other – for example, UNO or chess.

REAL-LIFE CONTEXT

A whole new world

Age range: all ages

What is it?

Can we make it real? Learning about materials? Go on a walk around the school and outside. Learning about taste buds? Bring in some food. Learning about artefacts? Create an excavation dig for them in tuff trays. How can we make the learning real?

When can I use it?

Wherever you can. Some lessons will lend themselves better. For example, for maths you will easily come up with ideas for symmetry, area, perimeter or shape!

Why does it work?

If you can make it physically tangible, children will feel that purpose and connection to what they are learning.

Steps

1   Think about the lesson and learning.
2   Is there a way it can be explored physically?
3   Get moving!

Simplify

It doesn't have to be bells and whistles. Simply using real-life objects such as leaves for arrays will support that connection.

Challenge

Utilise your parents and your community – for example, bringing parents in to talk about their culture or asking parents to bring their pets in.

JOURNEY LESSONS

Where are we going?

Age range: all ages

What is it?

Children are far more engaged when there's an end purpose. For example, are they creating books to read to younger children? Are they writing speeches to be presented to parents? Or posters to be stuck around school? Are they calculating the budget for the winter fair and creating the menu? Are they writing to pen pals in another country?

INTRINSIC

When can I use it?

There's not always going to be an elaborate grand purpose that links to the wider school. But think about what they are learning and how you could add an extra oomph to it by setting a goal to work towards.

Why does it work?

If you can make it physically tangible, children will feel that purpose and connection to what they are learning.

Steps

1   Think about the lesson and learning.
2   Is there an outcome that stretches beyond the classroom?
3   Connect with people who could support like other class teachers, parents, senior leaders who could help.

Simplify

Start with links that just make sense. For example, learning a song? Why not sing it altogether at pick-up time in front of the parents? Start with links that require little effort or planning!

Challenge

Have a regular lesson or subject that links to a purpose. For example, every handwriting lesson links to writing the menu for school dinners next week which are then delivered to classrooms.

CONNECTIONS

How does it link?

Age range: all ages

What is it?

Connect learning from different subjects together to strengthen the purpose.

INTRINSIC

When can I use it?

That is the beauty of connection. Start with your topic such as your history or geography focus and branch out. For example:

- the Stone Age
- Stone Age cave painting
- materials – clothes-making
- Stone Age diary
- Stone Age patterns and symmetry.

Why does it work?

When children experience the learning in different ways it strengthens their engagement with the topic, and they feel a sense of purpose within the curriculum.

Steps

1 Start with the topic.
2 Link to the writing.
3 Connect to the art.
4 Find other connections!

Simplify

Don't force it; if you can't link it to every subject that is totally fine!

Challenge

Cross-referencing this with the 'journey' can be super-impactful. For example, at the end of the journey we will create a stop-motion video all about the Stone Age.

THE MISSION

Storytelling strategy

Age range: all ages

What is it?

Setting up the learning as a secret mission taps into engagement and purpose. You can quite literally start with: 'Oh, my goodness! We have a secret mission today team.' For older children it might sound more like: 'We have a pretty big challenge today team. I feel like I need to take a breath before I share this with you.'

When can I use it?

At the beginning of a lesson to set out the learning in a storytelling context.

Why does it work?

It works because children love to feel like they are taking part in something big! Suddenly it isn't just another maths lesson. It is something they are all in together, it's a quest, it's a challenge!

Steps

1   Think about the lesson and the goal.
2   The magic is in the pitch, it is story time.
3   Pitch it as a challenge and sell it!

Simplify

Try these story starters:

Team, we have a mission today, should you choose to accept it!
Oh my gosh! I don't think anyone else could do this but (name of your class).
We have a big challenge ahead of us but I think we can do it!

Challenge

Why not have someone from another class come in and 'deliver' the mission.

THE MYSTERY

Storytelling strategy

Age range: all ages

What is it?

Set up the learning as a mystery to solve.

When can I use it?

It depends on the lesson, but I am sure we've all seen the classroom in chaos after Goldilocks has visited or a flour-shaped gingerbread man in the playground. For older learners it might be a mystery letter or a missing part of a textbook found on your head teacher's desk. It could also be a photo or a drawing, with the mystery being what it is.

Why does it work?

A mystery to solve? CLASSIC intrinsic motivation.

Steps

1   Think about how your lesson could be approached as a mystery.
2   It might be having the answer at the beginning.
3   It might be having the middle (subject knowledge) at the beginning.
4   Use prompt questions to engage children.

Simplify

When in doubt, start with an envelope.

Challenge

Combine your connections to solve the mystery! It might be to crack and decode across the week!

ONCE UPON A TIME

Storytelling strategy

Age range: all ages

What is it?

A tale as old as time. Literally. We are wired to feel connected to stories. Using a personal story that links to your lesson will increase your children's engagement.

INTRINSIC

When can I use it?

Authenticity is best. If you have a personal story, tell it! For example:
'I used to feel so confused about rounding, literally I would just be sitting in the lesson looking at my teacher and having no clue what to do. But then my dad taught me this trick and it has always stayed with me. Do you want to hear it?'

Why does it work?

Storytelling is a powerful tool that ignites many areas of our brains. When we listen to a story it taps into social contagion and a sense of community. Stories help to build schemas which support our processing and ability to retrieve information.

Steps

1   Start with a hook; make sure you use first person.
2   Tap into emotions as this will intrigue children.
3   Give personal details like the names of people in your life as this will feel exclusive!

Simplify

Try these story stems:

You might not know this about me, but …
You probably won't guess this, but …
This will surprise you, but …

Challenge

Add a photo before you start the story, so children are extra intrigued and have a visual while you are sharing your story. For example, it might be a photo of you from school.

CHAPTER 24
C IS FOR CONNECT

Classroom essentials

CONNECTION CUES

Five ways to boost connections every day

Let's start our connection manual with connection cues, signals of connection that support pupils to feel a sense of belonging throughout the day.

Greetings

Yep, it is greetings again! One of the most simple and effective ways to ensure children feel a sense of belonging. I would recommend doing it three times a day (morning, lunch and home time).

PROUD wall

Your children are in your classroom six hours a day. How do they feel connected? By being part of it! I always recommend every classroom to have a *proud wall* with an allocation for each child to display their proudest work.

Connection box

Heard of a worry box? Yep, this is better. A connection box is simply a letter box of some sort where children can write or draw to you. You choose what time of day children can do this and when you will check it. The idea is that you are not unreachable. This makes children feel more connected to you. Simply circling back to that note provides a valuable connection cue.

I noticed . . .

It is easy to say 'amazing', 'well done' and 'great job'. But when we notice our children specifically, they feel a connection boost. For example, 'I noticed you waiting'; 'I noticed you got a work bank'; 'I noticed you sharing'. This switch makes a big difference.

Story time

Regardless of the age of your children, story time is an important routine for connection. Stories activate several areas of the brain and are associated with community and positive emotions.

CONNECTION IN EVERY LESSON 1

Partner work

Connection cues are important because they ensure children are 'topped up' with a sense of belonging and safety throughout the day. But now let's look at how we can harness connection in every lesson through partner and group work. Both of these practices can be used in every lesson. This will embed a sense of community and accelerate a sense of engagement.

Partner talk: BIGG framework

Not just any partner talk will support connection. It needs to provide opportunities for discussion and a development of social skills. To perfect your partner talk we can use our TGMC framework 'BIGG'.

Partner talk: Better questions

If we want children to feel a sense of connection through partner talk, we need to ensure the question actually evokes a conversation. Before you ask it, think: is there enough to discuss?

Partner talk: Invite conversation

Encourage children to talk to each other, not blurt an answer out. There are two things we can do here:
First, expect children to decide who is talking first. We can do this simply by asking them to ask: 'Would you like to go first or should I?'

Second, we can give children a sentence starter to ensure they are developing their conversation skills. It might be 'I think this character is feeling xx'.

Gamify

Add a challenge or follow-up question on the board. This will support children to sustain conversation rather than lose engagement.

Group response

Once they have talked, AVOID hands up. This will kill engagement. Try summarising what you hear or using task don't ask strategies.

If we use partner talk every lesson, developing the social skills and opportunity for connection is well worth our time. Positive conversations will support children to feel more engaged with the lesson.

CONNECTION IN EVERY LESSON 2

Five ways to mix up your partner talk

Walk and talk

As you know, this is a firm favourite of mine! Have a signal for walking around the room (I like to use a reception bell), then the same signal for stopping and talking with a partner. Repeat two to three times.

Dominoes

From two to four to six. This is a great way to build confidence and community. Give children an opportunity to talk with their partner to identify their group of four on the carpet. You can then extend to a group of six! You will need to teach children these groups, but once embedded it is a great tool!

Only pictures

Have children discuss something with a partner, but they can only use pictures! This causes a great sense of fun and engagement. They can draw directly on the table or on whiteboards.

Only actions

Have children discuss something in partners, but they can only use actions! Again, children will love the element of play and it will certainly keep them engaged.

Only written words

Have children discuss something in partners, but they can only use written words! Perfect for older learners. You will have some lovely silent discussions!

CONNECTION IN EVERY LESSON 3

Group work

Group work is often avoided due to the classroom management side of things! But don't forget our routines section. You have the MAAT kit to ensure you succeed. Flick back to p. XX, Chapter 16, whenever you need to plan a group task. The more we make time for group work the more we develop engagement. There are seven group work tasks you can do in (pretty much) any lesson.

Graffiti

In groups, generate ideas, storyboard information, play-scripts; draw what you remember straight on a table. If your school doesn't allow that, flip chart paper and felt tips work a treat!

Puzzle

This one is back! Take a photo, illustration or text linked to the learning, cut it up and have children puzzle it back together. Link questions to the puzzle and they will be more invested in discussing!

Board game

Doesn't have to be reinventing the wheel. You can simply input questions to a snakes and ladders template. Use inspiration from our playful games manual to have children playing linked to the learning.

Tableau

Fancy name for a freeze frame! It basically means 'living picture'. Have children work in groups to represent a scene or an understanding of a concept.

Charades

Have children act out key parts of the learning for their group to guess. You can extent this and have children create their own charades cards, meaning they resource the activity too!

CONNECTION IN EVERY LESSON 4

Group work

Pictionary

Have children draw key parts of the learning for their group to guess. You can extend this and have children create their own Pictionary cards, meaning they resource the activity too!

Taboo

Have children explain key parts of the learning to their group to guess. Have words on the card that the children are unable to say! You can extend this and have children create their own taboo cards meaning they resource the activity too!

CHAPTER 25
A IS FOR ATTUNEMENT

CLASSROOM ESSENTIALS

ATTUNING YOUR TASKS

ATTUNEMENT

Let's activate!

What are activating strategies?

If our children are presenting low arousal levels/are under-responsive they would benefit from some activating strategies to ensure they can engage successfully with the task.

How do we know if our class needs activation?

If children have low arousal levels/are under-responsive we might see:

Lack of participation and discussion

eads slumped on desks

Restlessness and fidgeting

ACTIVATING BUFFERS

ATTUNEMENT

Activating buffers are short (under five-minute) tasks you can do with your class to dial up the energy. These can also be used individually where a child may need to activate!

Bunny breath

Three sharp inhales through the nose and an exhale through the mouth. Three times in a row. Stand up for extra activation!

Palm press

Stand up. Press your palms together and stretch your arms up to the sky. Wiggle your fingers for an extra wake-up.

Wall push

Go to a wall. Put two palms on it and PUSH for 30 seconds. Extend where needed.

Partner push

Put your palms together and push, gradually increasing the pressure.

Partner pull

Hold a partner's hand and slowly pull back, maintaining balance.

Interlocking clasp

Lock your hands like you're praying. Switch your finger position forwards and backwards slowly and then speed up the pace.

ACTIVATING ADAPTERS

These are ways you can adapt your task to match the energy levels of your children. If you feel children need more than a buffer, you might try one of these.

Instead of	Add some energy
Having children retell the story to their partner	Show six yoga poses on the board. Have children work together to retell the story using yoga poses

Partner talk ideas	Beach ball toss ideas

Asking children to write their ideas on a whiteboard or in their book

Use 'the scale' to get them to move and vote in the classroom first

A partner talk

A walk and talk

Doing their independent work at their desks

Take it outside!

ACTIVATING ADAPTERS (CONTINUED)

Instead of	Add some energy
Starting with a quiet task	Start with a song linked to the learning on YouTube! MC Grammar anyone!

Instead of	Add some energy
Having children sit and listen for the main teach	Use visual comprehension where they can draw what they understand on their whiteboard. Stop and share at regular intervals. You could even expand it into a walk and talk

Completing a worksheet linked to the learning

Turn it into a relay race

Completing a worksheet linked to the learning

Cut the worksheet up and turn it into an obstacle course

ATTUNING YOUR TASKS

ATTUNEMENT

Let's calm

What are calming strategies?

If our children are presenting high arousal levels or are over-responsive they would benefit from some calming strategies to ensure they can engage successfully with the task

How do we know if our class needs calming?

If children have high arousal levels/are over-responsive, we might see:

Lots of calling out

Lots of fidgeting and children out of sorts

Inability to start the task or focus

Calming buffers

Calming buffers are short (under five-minute) tasks you can do with your class to dial down the energy. These can also be used individually where a child needs them.

Finish the doodle

Draw a doodle on the board or directly on children's table and ask them to continue it.

Hug

Invite children to wrap their arms around their bodies and take deep breaths as they hug.

Rocks and socks

Take an inhale and tense your body, wrapping your arms around for a squeeze. As you exhale, flop like a sock.

Grounding strategy 5, 4, 3, 2, 1

Notice five things you can see; four things you can touch; three things you can hear; two things you can smell; and one thing you can taste.

Relaxing bodies

Take a moment of calm by utilising relaxing exercises like: rub your temples, squeeze your feet, make circles on your palms or squeeze your shoulders.

Reading

Silent reading for your older children or looking at picture books for younger children. Both create a sense of calm.

ATTUNING YOUR TASKS

Let's calm

Calming adapters

These are ways you can adapt your tasks to match the energy levels of your children. If you think children need more than a buffer, you might try one of these. In short, it is about making it independent to support decompression.

Instead of	Add some energy
Having children discuss what they learnt last lesson	Invite children to complete (or create) a crossword or wordsearch linked to the last lesson

r	e	a	d	P	u	y	s
g	i	f	b	v	e	j	n
i	P	n	o	w	b	n	o
s	c	h	o	o	l	P	e
y	w	l	k	r	f	g	t
h	o	m	e	k	s	t	i
t	i	m	e	a	z	m	r
h	c	q	u	d	r	a	w

1. read   4. draw   7. time
2. book   5. pen   8. school
3. write   6. work   9. home

Instead of	Add some energy
Doing a walk and talk	Give children a journal prompt at their tables

Creating a group project quiz

Invite children to create independent chatterbox quizzes

Recreating a chapter or section of a book through drama

Invite children to create a mini booklet or comic strip linked to the book

Scavenger hunt linked to the learning

Use play-dough to answer questions linked to the learning

CHAPTER 26
L IS FOR THE LADDER
Classroom essentials

BODY MAPPING

Preparing for resilience

LADDER

What is it?

A practical way to explore how feelings show up in our body.

Why it works

It is a concrete way to understanding how resilience feels. This supports children to recognise it, label it and be prepared for it.

When can I use it?

It is worth teaching children about this separately from the task. Children can create their own, perhaps after you have done a class example. Before a task with a challenge, you can bring it up to discuss.

EMOTIONAL VACCINES

Preparing for resilience

What is it?

This strategy is from Dr Becky Kennedy (2022). It basically involves talking about possible big feelings before an activity or event to problem-solve what they could do if it happens.

Why it works

Emotional vaccines take the shock out of feelings and prepare children with the tools they need at a time when they can comprehend it best.

When can I use it?

Before a task so children can think about what resilience might look and feel like.

What might it sound like?

'We have a big write this lesson. Sometimes it can feel tricky when you aren't sure what to write next. This is a great opportunity for resilience. How could we move forward if we didn't know what to write?' Generate ideas and this becomes your resilience toolkit.

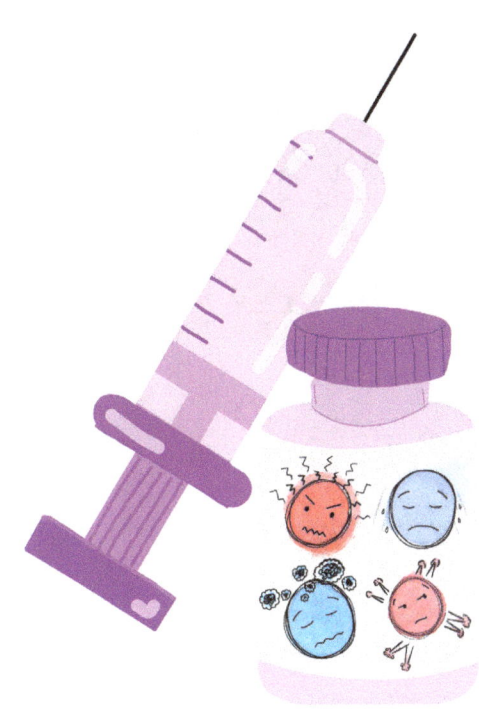

RESILIENCE TOOLKIT

Resilience ready!

What is it?

Tangible ideas for children to use when they need it most! It could be a physical toolbox in class where you put things in and discuss it after emotional vaccines or it could be a teaching slide. This could be linked to the learning or linked to emotional support. You choose based on what you have and the needs of your class. Here are some ideas . . .

Ear defenders

Toolbox

Multiplication chart

X	0	1	2	3	4	5	6	7	8	9	10	11	12
0	0	0	0	0	0	0	0	0	0	0	0	0	0
1	0	1	2	3	4	5	6	7	8	9	10	11	12
2	0	2	4	6	8	10	12	14	16	18	20	22	24
3	0	3	6	9	12	15	18	21	24	27	30	33	36
4	0	4	8	12	16	20	24	28	32	36	40	44	48
5	0	5	10	15	20	25	30	35	40	45	50	55	60
6	0	6	12	18	24	30	36	42	48	54	60	66	72
7	0	7	14	21	28	35	42	49	56	63	70	77	84
8	0	8	16	24	32	40	48	56	64	72	80	88	96
9	0	9	18	27	36	45	54	63	72	81	90	99	108
10	0	10	20	30	40	50	60	70	80	90	100	110	120
11	0	11	22	33	44	55	66	77	88	99	110	121	132
12	0	12	24	36	48	60	72	84	96	108	120	132	144

Look back in your book

Numberline

Numicon

Fidget

Interactive idea wall

Sound button

Quiet seat

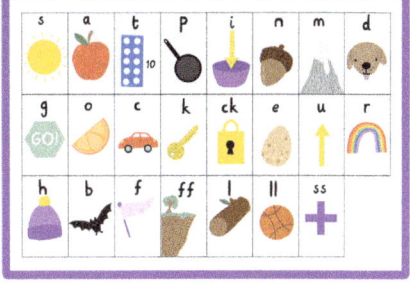

Word mat

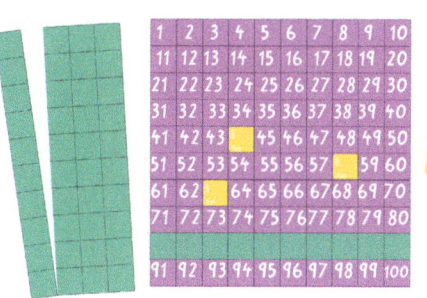

Base 10

WHOLE CLASS PATHWAYS™

The more we see our growth, the more we grow

LADDER

What is it?

A signature TGMC strategy, Whole Class Pathways is about chunking the learning into manageable steps and normalising bumps or 'obstacles' along the way.

Why it works

It makes growth mindset and resilience a story that we all experience rather than something horrible that is only happening to us. It creates a sense of community and an excitement about problem-solving rather than a need to shut down when things get tricky.

How will we get there?

Learn

1st stop

How can we bridge so

Obstacles happen!

How do I implement it?

Identify your collaborative learning goal for the lesson and make it the destination

Identify the 'stops' along the way, i.e. the micro steps to achieving it

Talk about possible obstacles that could stop them moving forward

Generate ideas for how you could 'bridge' this, supporting that resilience toolkit

athways

stop

3rd stop

What is our destination?

PERSONAL PATHWAYS™

The more we see our growth, the more we grow

What is it?

A personal adaptation of our signature TGMC strategy, this involves creating a responsive pathway for an individual pupil when needed.

Why it works

It creates a bespoke resilience toolkit for them. It identifies how to personally move forward on the spot. The visual pathway enables them to view their learning as a journey. The destination and stops are made individual to that child so they can achieve success. Each time they move forward it shows then that they can do it, which develops their mindset and resilience.

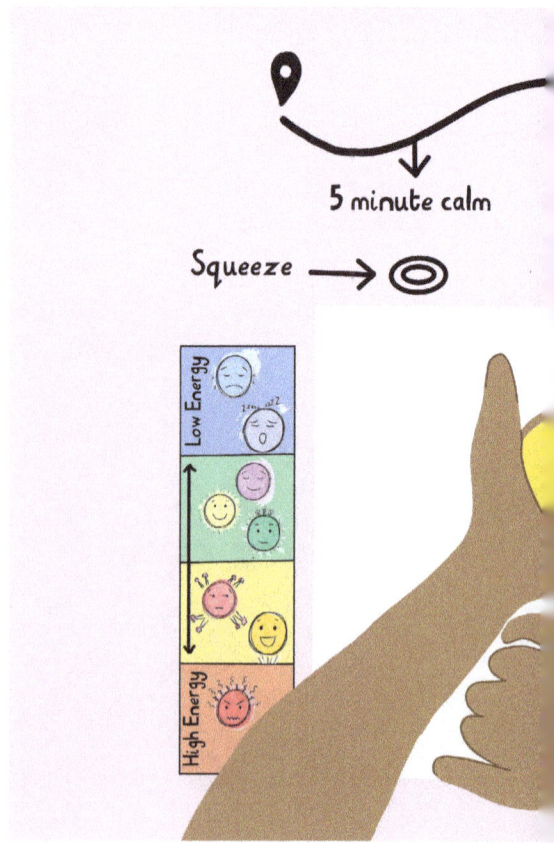

How do I implement it?

It creates a bespoke resilience toolkit for them. It identifies how to personally move forward on the spot. The visual pathway enables them to view their learning as a journey. The destination and stops are made individual to that child so they can achieve success. Each time they move forward it shows them that they can do it which develops their mindset and resilience.

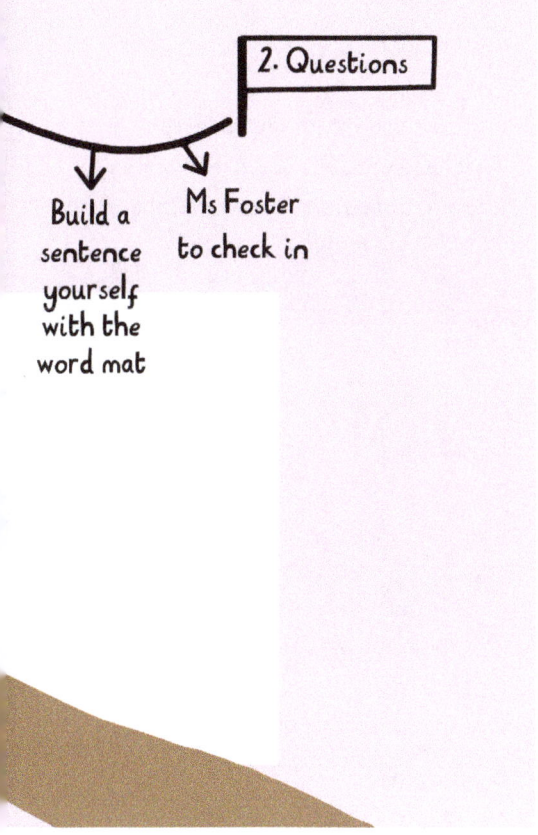

STRUGGLE SCRIPTS

What can we say?

What is it?

What can we say as the educator when we see a child struggling?

> This feels tricky hey? Okay, we prepared for this, what can we do?
>
> *Looking at the resilience toolkit*

Why it works

It repeats the same message, supporting consistency and understanding.

> Have you hit an obstacle? Ooh, it feels tough, but you are learning something new. This is exciting. How could we bridge the obstacle?

When can I use it?

Instead of 'you can do it' or doing it for them

> It is hard to be resilient. I feel it too. What can we grab from our resilience toolkit?

AFFIRMATIONS

Let's rewire

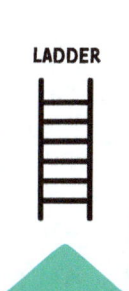

What is it?

Positive phrases for children to say about themselves and to themselves.

Why it works

It rewires negative narratives and over time develops a growth mindset.

When can I use it?

It is helpful to have an 'affirmation of the week', so children can repeat the same phrase and unpick what it means.

I am... a problem solver

PRE-TASKS

Ready, set . . .

What is it?

A task similar to their independent talk that they can do on whiteboards or with a partner first.

Why it works

It builds confidence. When you take time to reflect on what they have done, it supports their mindset for the independent task. It transitions what could feel like a big jump.

Examples

- The first two sentences of a big write on their whiteboard or straight on their desk.
- The first two questions with a partner on a whiteboard.

WIN SCRIPTS

Let's build connections

What is it?

Created by play therapist Ginny Magee, WIN scripts are an alternative to generic praise.

I saw you want to get some base 10. What were you thinking when you did that? This is what I call resilient!

Why it works

It focuses on the effort and the skills instead of the outcome, which is reinforced by Carol Dweck (2014) as a way to develop a growth mindset.

I saw you took a grounding break. What reminded you to do that?

Great resilience!

WIN scripts

W – witness
I – invite
N – name

I noticed you looking back in your book. How did you keep going when it felt tricky?

I love your resilience!

GROUNDING BREAK

Normalise a re-set

What is it?

When we are in the thick of it, we might go for a walk, call a friend, take a moment. These are ways we keep going, not give up. We need to normalise this for our children by sharing a way they can have a grounding break.

Why it works

It acknowledges that big feelings happen when you are being resilient and provides a practical way to support themselves.

GROWTH BOOKMARK

LADDER

Let achievements take up space

What is it?

A way for children to reflect on the achievements they are really proud of by recording them on a bookmark.

Why it works

It gives children a reminder from them to them about what they can do when they push forward.

When can I use it?

Initiated by the child. I would recommend everyone having a growth bookmark or having a page at the back of their books!

16.12.24

I didn't give up! I used numicon and finished my work. YAY!

RESILIENCE STEPS™

Talking about growth

What is it?

A TGMC visual to show how our mindset impacts our progress.

I want

I can't do it!

I won't do it!

Why it works

It makes something very abstract like 'mindset' visually concrete. It also supports children to move one step at a time.

How to use it

Use as a visual on your classroom on tables. When children are stuck or seemingly not moving forward, ask them 'Which step are you on right now?' 'How could we move forward?' 'What could help us?'

I did it!

I will do it!

I can do it!

I try to do it.

do it?

References

Allen, B., Ford, I., Hallahan, G. and Hannay, T. (2024) *Teacher Recruitment and Retention in 2024*. Available at: www.gatsby.org.uk/uploads/education/2024-06-13-teacher-tapp-final-teacher-recruitment-and-retention-in-2024.pdf (accessed: 11 January 2025).

Barrett, L.F. (2021) *Seven and a Half Lessons About the Brain*. London: Picador.

Berry, A. (2022) *Reimagining Student Engagement: From Disrupting to Driving*. Thousand Oaks, CA: Corwin.

Bethune, A. (2023) *Wellbeing in the Primary Classroom: The Updated Guide to Teaching Happiness and Positive Mental Health*. London: Bloomsbury Education.

Bottrill, G. (2022) *Can I Go And Play Now?: Rethinking the Early Years*. London: Corwin.

British Red Cross (2020) *Life After Lockdown: Tackling Loneliness.* Available at: www.redcross.org.uk/about-us/what-we-do/we-speak-up-for-change/life-after-lockdown-tackling-loneliness (accessed: 10 January 2025).

Brown, S. and Vaughan, C. (2010) *Play: How It Shapes the Brain, Opens the Imagination, and Invigorates the Soul*. New York: Avery.

Bryce-Clegg, A. and Silverton, K. (2023) Episode 2: Tips for managing emotional responses with Kate Silverton, *Early Years Podcast*. Available at: https://worldofeducation.tts-group.co.uk/episode-2-practical-tips-for-managing-emotional-responses-with-kate-silverton/ (accessed: 10 January 2025).

Busch, B. (2024) Make the best of wait times in your classroom, *InnerDrive*. Available at: www.innerdrive.co.uk/blog/wait-times-in-your-classroom/ (accessed: 10 January 2025).

Christakis, N.A. and Fowler, J.H. (2011) *Connected: The Amazing Power of Social Networks And How They Shape Our Lives*. London: HarperPress.

Clear, J. (2018) *Atomic Habits: An Easy and Proven Way to Build Good Habits and Break Bad Ones: Tiny Changes, Remarkable Results*. New York: Avery.

Clear, J. (2020) *How Long Does it Actually Take to Form a New Habit? (Backed by Science)*. Available at: https://jamesclear.com/new-habit (accessed: 10 January 2025).

Committee of Public Accounts (2023) *Education Recovery in Schools in England*. Available at: https://publications.parliament.uk/pa/cm5803/cmselect/cmpubacc/998/report.html (accessed: 11 January 2025).

Conway, J. (2024) Rewiring how neurodiversity is taught in the classroom, *Edinburgh Impact*. Available at: https://impact.ed.ac.uk/research/future-health-and-care/rewiring-how-neurodiversity-is-taught-in-the-classroom/ (accessed: 11 January 2025).

Coyle, D. (2019) *The Culture Code: The Secrets of Highly Successful Groups*. London: Random House.

Csikszentmihalyi, M. (1975) *Beyond Boredom and Anxiety: Experiencing Flow in Work and Play*. San Francisco: Jossey-Bass.

Daywalt, D. (2014) *The Day the Crayons Quit*. London: HarperCollins.

Dearybury, J. and Jones, J. (2020) *The Playful Classroom: The Power of Play for All Ages*. Hoboken, NJ: Jossey-Bass.

Department for Education (DfE) (2019) *Early Career Framework*. Available at: https://assets.publishing.service.gov.uk/media/60795936d3bf7f400b462d74/Early-Career_Framework_April_2021.pdf (accessed: 29 January 2025).

DfE (2021) *Teachers' Standards: Guidance for School Leaders, School Staff and Governing Bodies*. Available at: https://assets.publishing.service.gov.uk/media/61b73d6c8fa8f50384489c9a/Teachers__Standards_Dec_2021.pdf (accessed: 29 January 2025).

DfE (2024) *Statistics: Special Educational Needs (SEN)*. Available at: www.gov.uk/government/collections/statistics-special-educational-needs-sen (accessed: 10 January 2025).

Dix, P. (2017) *When the Adults Change Everything Changes: Seismic Shifts in School Behaviour*. Carmarthen: Independent Thinking Press.

Duckworth, A. (2013) Grit: The power of passion and perseverance, *TEDTalk*. Available at: www.youtube.com/watch?v=H14bBuluwB8 (accessed: 10 January 2025).

Dweck, C. (2014) The power of believing that you can improve, *TEDTalk*. Available at: www.youtube.com/watch?v=_X0mgOOSpLU (accessed: 10 January 2025).

Dweck, C.S. (2007) *Mindset: The New Psychology of Success: How We Can Learn to Fulfill Our Potential*. New York: Random House.

experianta (n.d.) Mehrabian's 7/38/55 model. Available at: https://experianta.com/directory/concepts/mehrabians-communication-theory/(accessed: 19 February 2025).

Explore-Blog (2013) 1975 comic on the factory model of education, *Tumblr*. Available at: https://explore.themarginalian.org/post/68017070197/this-1975-comic-on-the-factory-model-of-education (accessed: 11 January 2025).

Fábrega, A.L. (2023) *The Learning Game: Teaching Kids to Think for Themselves, Embrace Challenge, and Love Learning*. Petersfield: Harriman House.

Fisher, D., Frey, N., Quaglia, R.J., Smith, D. and Lande, L.L. (2018) *Engagement by Design: Creating Learning Environments Where Students Thrive*. Thousand Oaks, CA: Corwin.

French, B. (2023) *Kids Do Better When They are Excited to Learn*. Available at: https://teachbetter.com/blog/kids-do-better-when-they-are-excited-to-learn/ (accessed: 11 January 2025).

Gerlach, J. (2023) The curious mind: A key to mental wellness, *Psychology Today*. Available at: www.psychologytoday.com/intl/blog/beyond-mental-health/202309/the-curious-mind-a-key-to-mental-wellness (accessed: 10 January 2025).

Griffin, K. (2023) *Success with Sensory Supports: The Ultimate Guide to Using Sensory Diets, Movement Breaks, and Sensory Circuits at School*. London: Jessica Kingsley.

Gruber, M. (2015) *This is Your Brain on Curiosity*. Available at: www.youtube.com/watch?v=SmaTPPB-T_s (accessed: 10 January 2025).

Hari, J. (2023) *Stolen Focus: Why You Can't Pay Attention*. London: Bloomsbury.

Hepburn, E. (2023) *A Toolkit for Your Emotions: 45 Ways to Feel Better*. London: Greenfinch.

Hrach, S. (2021) *Minding Bodies: How Physical Space, Sensation, and Movement Affect Learning*. Morgantown: West Virginia University Press.

Immordino-Yang, M.H. (2015) *Emotions, Learning and the Brain: Exploring the Educational Implications of Affective Neuroscience*. London: W.W. Norton & Co.

Immordino-Yang, M.H. and Damasio, A.R. (2007) We feel, therefore we learn: The relevance of affective and social neuroscience to education. *Mind, Brain and Education*, 1(1), 3–10. *Reprinted in *Jossey-Bass Reader on the Brain and Learning*. San Francisco: Jossey-Bass, pp. 183–98.

Kennedy, B. (2022) *Good Inside: A Guide to Becoming the Parent You Want to Be*. London: HarperCollins.

Kohn, A. (2018) *Punished by Rewards: The Trouble with Gold Stars, Incentive Plans, A's, Praise, and Other Bribes*. Boston: Houghton Mifflin.

Kuypers, L. (2011) *The Zones of Regulation: A Curriculum to Foster Self-Regulation*. Cambridge: Think Social.

Kuypers, L. (2024) What are the four zones of regulation? *The Zones of Regulation*. Available at: https://zonesofregulation.com/what-are-the-four-zones-of-regulation/ (accessed: 10 January 2025).

Lemov, D. (2010) *II. 'No Opt Out': Four Techniques from 'Teach Like a Champion'*. Available at: https://4tlacstrategies.weebly.com/ii-no-opt-out.html (accessed: 11 January 2025).

Lewis, H. (2015) A hands up culture: Does it help behaviour? *LinkedIn*. Available at: www.linkedin.com/pulse/hands-up-culture-does-help-behaviour-huw-lewis-mbe/ (accessed: 11 January 2025).

Mediaofficer (2023) Why is school attendance so important and what are the risks of missing a day? *The Education Hub*. Available at: https://educationhub.blog.gov.uk/2023/05/school-attendance-important-risks-missing-day/ (accessed: 11 January 2025).

Naish, S. and Dillon, S. (2020) *The Quick Guide to Therapeutic Parenting: A Visual Introduction*. London: Jessica Kingsley.

Nip in the Bud (2023) *Barriers to Learning: Why Children Might Not be Engaged at School*. Available at: https://nipinthebud.org/blog/barriers-to-learning-why-children-might-not-be-engaged-at-school/ (accessed: 11 January 2025).

Pink, D.H. (2011) *Drive: The Surprising Truth About What Motivates Us*. New York: Riverhead.

Place2Be (2024) *Parenting Smart: De-escalation Techniques with Children*. Available at: https://parentingsmart.place2be.org.uk/article/de-escalation-techniques-with-children (accessed: 10 January 2025).

Radhakrishnan, G. (2023) How walking boosts creative thinking: Lessons from Steve Jobs and Stanford, *Medium*. Available at: https://medium.com/@gowrishankar005/how-walking-boosts-creative-thinking-lessons-from-steve-jobs-and-stanford-dfe277c2bd22 (accessed: 11 January 2025).

Raichlen, D. (2024) Podcast notes and takeaways for: The brain professor: 'Popular treat now considered deadlier than smoking!', 'Running on a treadmill is making you depressed!' *The Diary of A CEO*, *PodPulse*. Available at: https://podpulse.ai/podcast-notes-and-takeaways/the-diary-of-a-ceo-the-brain-professor-popular-treat-now-considered-deadlier-than-smoking-running-on-a-treadmill-is-making-you-depressed-david-raichlen (accessed: 11 January 2025).

Reese, D.D., Pawluk, D.T.V. and Taylor, C.R. (2016) Engaging learners through rational design of multisensory effects. In Tettegah, S. and Noble, S. (eds), *Emotions, Technology, and Design*. London: Academic Press, pp. 103–27.

Robinson, K. (2018) Ken Robinson: creativity and curiosity, *YouTube*. Available at: https://youtu.be/CbiP3rc63LE (accessed: 10 January 2025).

Rosen, M. (2016) *We're Going on a Bear Hunt*. London: Walker Books.

Rudy, L.J. (2024) Why do autistic children stim? *Verywell Health*. Available at: www.verywellhealth.com/what-is-stimming-in-autism-260034 (accessed: 11 January 2025).

Salih, T. (2025) *The Adaptive Teaching Planner*. Available at: https://inclusion-teacher.com/product/adaptive-teaching-planner-soft-cover-a4/ (accessed: 19 February 2025).

Seligman, M. (2011) *Flourish: A New Understanding of Happiness and Wellbeing: The Practical Guide to Using Positive Psychology to Make You Happier and Healthier*. London: Nicholas Brealey.

Selk, J. (2021) Habit formation: The 21-day myth, *Forbes*. Available at: www.forbes.com/sites/jasonselk/2013/04/15/habit-formation-the-21-day-myth/ (accessed: 11 January 2025).

Shah, P.E., Weeks, H.M., Richards, B. and Kaciroti, N. (2018) Early childhood curiosity and kindergarten reading and math academic achievement. *Paediatric Research*, 84(3), 380–6. https://doi.org/10.1038/s41390-018-0039-3

Sherrington, T. (2022) Hands up! When it's helpful and when it's not, *teacherhead*. Available at: https://teacherhead.com/2022/11/06/hands-up-when-its-helpful-and-when-its-not/ (accessed: 11 January 2025).

Sobel, D. and Alston, S. (2021) *The Inclusive Classroom: A New Approach to Differentiation*. London: Bloomsbury Education.

Stenger, M. (2014) Why curiosity enhances learning, *Edutopia*. Available at: www.edutopia.org/blog/why-curiosity-enhances-learning-marianne-stenger (accessed: 11 January 2025).

TES (2024) Behaviour: What UK educators could expect this year. Available at: www.tes.com/en-gb/for-schools/blog/article/behaviour-what-uk-educators-could-expect-year (accessed: 28 January 2025).

The Diary of A CEO (2024) The exercise neuroscientist: NEW RESEARCH, the shocking link between exercise and dementia! Available at: www.youtube.com/watch?v=5o-tRub-0pQ (accessed: 10 January 2025).

Thoonsen, M. and Lamp, C. (2021) *Sensory Solutions in the Classroom: The Teacher's Guide to Fidgeting, Inattention and Restlessness*. London: Jessica Kingsley.

Treasure, J. (n.d.) 5 ways to listen better, *TEDTalk*. Available at: www.youtube.com/watch?v=3XyyJOB5eoQ Available at: (accessed: 19 February 2025).

Van Edwards, V. (2017) You are contagious, *TedX Talk*. Available at: www.youtube.com/watch?v=cef35Fk7YD8 (accessed: 29 January 2025).

ONLINE RESOURCES

fiveminutemum.com
playfullearninggames.co.uk

CHAPTER 22 LINKS

www.playfullearninggames.co.uk/blog/three-in-a-row-grammar-game/
www.playfullearninggames.co.uk/blog/remove-the-multiples/
www.playfullearninggames.co.uk/games/playful-tuff-tray-ideas-for-ks2/

MAGICAL ENGAGEMENT WHEEL

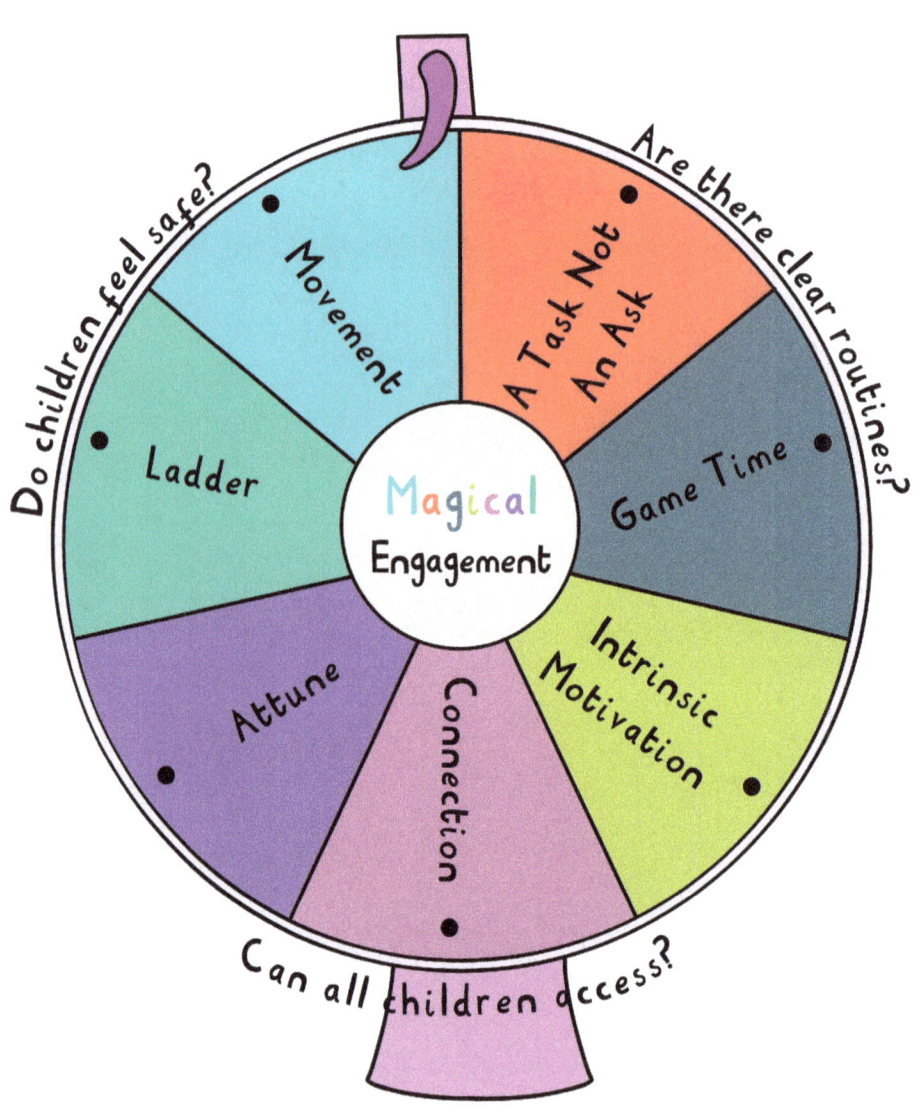

Index